Aspects of American Film History Prior to 1920

by

ANTHONY SLIDE

The Scarecrow Press, Inc.
Metuchen, N.J. & London
1978

Books by Anthony Slide:

Early American Cinema (1970)
The Griffith Actresses (1973)
The Idols of Silence (1976)
The Big V (1976)
Early Women Directors (1977)

With Edward Wagenknecht:

The Films of D. W. Griffith (1975)

Library of Congress Cataloging in Publication Data

Slide, Anthony.
    Aspects of American Film history prior to 1920.

    Bibliography: p.
    Includes index.
    1. Moving-pictures--United States--History--
Addresses, essays, lectures. 2. Silent films--
History--Addresses, essays, lectures. I. Title.
PN1993.5.U6S54   791.43'0973   78-2912
ISBN 0-8108-1130-8

For Bob Gitt, Ethel Grandin and Herb Sterne
With remembrance and anticipation of our
weekend screenings

CONTENTS

FOREWORD

Though I appreciate the compliment, I have no idea why Anthony Slide asked me to write an introduction to his new book, for he certainly does not need my attestation, and he knows a great deal more about many of the subjects he deals with than I do. But I agree with him wholeheartedly that this is just the kind of spadework that needs to be done before the real history of American film can ever be written, and I rejoice in whatever brings back the memory of how good movies can be in these, the sad days of their lamentable decline.

My only advantage over Tony is that because I was born long before he was, I saw a great many films which he knows only by repute. Of course I have forgotten most of them, but I have not forgotten how I felt about them, and it helps to have been a part of the times and to have experienced the enthusiasm which these pictures generated when they first appeared. I wrote The Movies in the Age of Innocence precisely because I wished to bear that kind of direct, eye-witness testimony. Very few film historians have the imagination needed to think themselves back into pre-World War I days. Tony is one of them, perhaps the outstanding one, and I can always achieve a meeting of minds with him, even when we chance to disagree about a particular film or personality.

In reading his book, I do not know whether to be more grateful to him for reminding me of the Kalem films I loved (especially The Colleen Bawn) or of, say, the exquisite loveliness of Florence LaBadie (I spent part of my Christmas in 1912 watching her radiant young Madonna in The Star of Bethlehem, and Thanhouser in general meant more to me than any other of the early independent companies), or for the chapters in which he deals, among other things, with players whom I either did not see or have forgotten and of some directors of whom I was unconscious as such, even though I saw a good many of their films. If Chapters 6 and 13 are the most amusing in his book, certainly the one on

Ethel Grandin is the most winning, and even though I have a print of <u>Traffic in Souls,</u> it leaves me wishing that I might have seen more than I did of that charming lady.

Edward Wagenknecht

West Newton, Mass.
June 5, 1977

"A sigh for the good old nights when a nickel--
or, to be luxurious, a dime--brought one into
personal contact with short works by E. S.
Porter, or Mack Sennett, or Colin Campbell,
or Tom Ince, or David Griffith. And in those
one- or two-reelers behold, sprinkled everywhere with the prodigality of heaven's dew,
Walthall, or Mabel Normand, or the Gish
miniatures or Blanche Sweet--even those gold-
en objects, Mary Pickford and Charlie Chaplin."--Photoplay, November, 1916.

INTRODUCTORY NOTE

This slim volume of essays will, I hope, supplement my first book on the pioneering years of the American film industry, Early American Cinema. I have tried to record here many of the lesser-known aspects of the American cinema prior to 1920; the work of forgotten film companies such as Thanhouser and Paralta, the evolution of the star system, the first child actors of the screen, etc. This is not a book for the casual browser who has only a slight interest in film history. I have assumed that my reader has a fairly detailed knowledge of the American film industry, and that my research will take him or her into nooks and crannies of the industry's past that have not been visited in recent years by other film historians.

I am aware that through the years my books and periodical articles have come to deal with more and more obscure subjects. I make no apologies for this. I rather delight in it. I do not believe I will ever write a general history of the cinema. In fact, at this point of time, I feel it unwise of any historian or scholar, however knowledgeable, to undertake such a task. President John Adams, in 1807, commented that a complete history of the American Revolution could not be written until all the state histories were known. It is my firm belief that much the same statement could be applied to the history of the American cinema today. There can be no complete history until the work of every company, however obscure, every technician, and every actor has been examined and recorded.

There is one publication, Films in Review, which has through the years attempted to do just this. It has become fashionable in certain circles to sneer at Films in Review; as one wit had it, the magazine knew the credits of everything and the value of nothing. That is an evaluation that I do not accept. When the definitive history of the cinema comes to be written, one of the basic resources will be, and must be, Films in Review.

It is my sincere wish that this book will encourage others to study further the early years of the cinema in this country. If, through my writings, a young scholar is persuaded to undertake, say, a detailed history of the Balboa Company of Long Beach or of director Oscar Apfel, then the years I have spent researching at the Library of Congress and in the libraries of the British Film Institute, the Museum of Modern Art, and the Academy of Motion Picture Arts and Sciences will not have been in vain.

Anthony Slide
Los Angeles
May 1977

1. THE EVOLUTION OF THE FILM STAR*

In the beginning there were no stars. Of course, from time to time stars from other fields of endeavor, such as the sports arena or the stage, were featured, but there were no film stars per se. Possibly the first film actor to be recognized by the trade press was Ben Turpin of Essanay. An article, "Life of a Moving Picture Comedian," appeared under his name in the April 3, 1909 issue of The Moving Picture World, in which Turpin commented, "This is a great life. I have been in the moving picture biz working for The Essanay for two years, and I must say I had many a good fall, and many ... a good bump, and I think I have broken about twenty barrels of dishes, upset stores, and also broken up many sets of beautiful furniture, had my eyes blackened, both ankles sprained and many bruises, and I am still on the go. This is a great business." As this obviously studio-written article illustrates, the cinema was very much in its infancy in terms of writing for its "fans."

The Moving Picture World was to continue to give prominence to film actors, but only gradually. Pearl White was the subject of an article on December 3, 1910, and three weeks later a full page was devoted to Mary Pickford, one of the first players generally recognized by the public even before her name was listed or known. By 1911, the journal had stories on actresses who were temporarily forced to retire from the screen for one reason or another. For example, in the February 4 issue appeared the following: "Little Bebe Daniels, the well-known professional child actress, lately appearing in Bison stock, has given up picture work for the present, and is now attending the Dominican Sacred Heart School. Those who have observed the child's work in the picture concede for her a brilliant future when she leaves the school and again takes up dramatic work."

---

*This essay was first published in a somewhat different format in Films in Review (December 1974).

Ben Turpin

Before entering films, many players had appeared in the illustrated song slides, popular in the pre-teens, for which they received no recognition whatsoever. Audiences seeing such slides in nickelodeons or vaudeville houses were totally unaware that the young girl proclaiming "I'd Rather Be on Broadway with You" was Alice Joyce, or that it was Mabel Normand asking "Is There Anything Else That I Can Do for You?" Francis X. Bushman received no billing as "Sailor Boy" or as the young man beseeching "Take Me Out to the End of the Pier." The fame of such performers in song slides, who also included Priscilla Dean, Ethel Grandin, Helene Chadwick, Florence La Badie, Anna Q. Nilsson and Anita Stewart, was assured by their acceptance of steady work in the motion picture industry.

Much has been made of stage actors' concern that their screen work be kept secret. Henry B. Walthall in a 1915 Photoplay interview claimed to have been shocked at discovering that James Kirkwood was appearing in films in 1909. Also in 1909, when Selig director Francis Boggs offered Hobart Bosworth the leading role in In the Power of the Sultan, Bosworth was apparently "heartily indignant," and was only willing to accept the role on condition that his name was not publicized. Did these so-called legitimate actors really care that much? I doubt it. The majority of actors who accepted screen roles were thankful not only for the work, but also for the fame it promised them. As Robert Grau points out in his 1914 volume, The Theatre of Science, the bulk of players employed in the film industry came not from the ranks of leading actors on the Broadway stage, not even from the ranks of Broadway's supporting players, but from provincial stock companies. As a typical example, Grau chose John Bunny, who had started with Vitagraph in 1910. "Bunny had been an actor for twenty-six years. His average salary was about $100 a week. He had been often promised more than this, but so unstable was the business procedure and often the engagements were so short and so varied that Bunny fairly jumped at the chance to enter the film which he had observed closely, and as he put it himself, 'Either I must make good on the screen or else starve to death....'" It was most certainly not starvation which killed John Bunny at the height of his screen fame in 1915.

There were certainly no complaints by members of the Kalem stock company as their identities were revealed in January 1910, when Kalem announced a "new method of lobby advertising." This new method was the issuance of posters and stills depicting the players with their names emblazoned beneath. Kalem's action was soon followed by Vitagraph, which not only released publicity material on its players but encouraged their personal appearances at neighborhood theatres. In April 1910, Florence Turner, "The Vitagraph Girl," appeared on stage at Brooklyn's Saratoga Park Moving Picture Parlor, and invited the audience to sing as the words of a song named in her honor were flashed on the screen.

Around this time, Frank E. Woods established the Moving Picture Department in The New York Dramatic Mirror. With an article titled "Why Is a Star?" in the October 1919 issue of Photoplay, Woods offered possibly the first serious consideration of the star system in the American film industry. He recalled, "Several Lizzies wrote to me wanting to know about the Vitagraph Girl, or the Biograph Girl, or whether Mr. and Mrs. Jones [characters portrayed by John Compson and Florence Lawrence in Biograph productions] were really married or not, or if Broncho Billy had a wife, before I took serious notice. Then I answered in the columns of the paper and the lid was off. It was the commencement of the Question and Answer Department, the predecessor of that most entertaining section of the Photoplay Magazine, the Answer Man."

The lid was indeed off; film players now realized that they had "fans." They realized that what they did, and even what they said, was important to millions of people. They understood what it was like to be a "star." Suddenly Constance and Norma Talmadge, Mary Fuller, Blanche Sweet, Anita Stewart, Alice Joyce, Clara Kimball Young, Maurice Costello, Billy Quirk and many, many others were no longer film players, but film stars. The film industry would never be the same again.

Variety of November 21, 1913 gloomily noted in a headline, "Picture Actors Are Asking for Names on the Screen." The article continued, "Film actors are scrapping for the spotlight. Printing the cast of the leading principals of the multiples and leaving the rest of the film mummers out of the lists is causing trouble. The film directors and executives are now going through the experiences of Broadway impresarios of regular productions in attempts to pacify players who want their names mentioned first as well as those who insist that if so-and-so's name is in big type theirs must be, too."

By 1915, these one-time stock company players had reached dizzy heights. Some--Helen Gardner, Florence Lawrence and Marion Leonard, for example--created their own producing companies. Mary Pickford and Charles Chaplin were demanding--and getting--astronomical salaries. Many had become overbearingly pompous. Variety (May 21, 1915) reported that film stars were refusing to take lower billing than stage stars, and cited this reason for Francis X. Bushman severing his contract with Essanay. Lottie Briscoe canceled her contract with Lubin because "Lubin called upon Miss Briscoe to assume a role which would have been the 'third party' of the film play. Resting upon her prerogative as a picture star, the girl declined to submit to the assignment, upon the ground it would be ill-fitting her position in the picture world to play secondary or thirdly to anyone of her sex."

It is worthwhile examining the attitude of the Biograph Company, the one producer which steadfastly refused to reveal the identities of its players--or so we are led to believe. There was no secrecy involved when the company signed an actor. In The Moving Picture World of February 25, 1911, there is a lengthy article concerning the Biograph actresses, Dorothy Bernard and Florence Barker. Dorothy Bernard is described as "one of the most talked-about actresses in the world." How could this be if the names of the Biograph players were unknown? When Mae Marsh resigned from the Kalem Company and rejoined the Biograph, her return was noted in The Moving Picture World of September 21, 1912. If not in life, at least in death, certainly, Biograph players received their rewards. When Vernon Clarges, a member of the Biograph's stock company, died on August 11, 1911, The Moving Picture World published an obituary notice which included the titles of several of his films.

In England, the Biograph Company's distributor, M. P. Sales, was forced to invent names for the Biograph players.* Blanche Sweet became Daphne Wayne, while Mack Sennett was Walter Terry. Some of the choices of names are rather curious; Robert Harron does look as if he might be a Willie McBain, although Mabel Normand is hardly a Muriel Fortescue!

---

*For a complete listing of such names, see this author's The Griffith Actresses (New York: A. S. Barnes, 1973).

I am convinced that by 1912 the names of the Biograph players were known to American audiences. In its issue of October 5 of that year, The Moving Picture World names Henry B. Walthall as the leading man of Friends and Two Daughters of Eve. In its issue of November 9, Blanche Sweet is noted as the star of The Painted Lady. Both Sweet and Walthall are mentioned in the February 22, 1913 review of Oil and Water. On April 22, 1913, The Moving Picture World announced a change in Biograph policy: "This week posters were issued bearing photographs and names of about a score of the members of the acting department of that organization." It was really too late; the bulk of the Biograph players were about to depart, along with director D. W. Griffith.

With the development of the actor into the film star, there had arisen a nostalgia for the past. That nostalgia which today creates stars of undistinguished players was as alive in the 'teens as it is today. By 1918, Sue Roberts was asking, in Motion Picture Magazine, of Walter Miller and King Baggott, "Where Have They Gone?" Miss Roberts also reported that "Lottie Briscoe's cinemic shade flittered away into ethereal nothingness."

Apparently, not only had the film star been born, but also that saccharine style of writing, so peculiarly belonging to the fan magazines, was fully launched.

2. COMEDIENNES OF THE 'TEENS

In the years prior to 1920, film comediennes came in all shapes and sizes. There was the buxom, domineering mother-in-law variety, exemplified by Louise Carver and Phyllis Allen. There was lanky, spinsterish Flora Finch, and there was young but grotesquely ugly Gale Henry. Cute, fat and lovable describes Marie Dressler, who never really came into her own in films until the arrival of sound and the series of features with Polly Moran for M-G-M, although she had starred in a number of 'teens comedies, including Tillie's Punctured Romance (1914), The Blacklist (1916) and Tillie Wakes Up (1917). Polly Moran, of course, had starred in the totally forgotten, but by all accounts quite excellent, "Sheriff Nell" series for Mack Sennett-Paramount in the late 'teens.

To many of these comediennes, the film industry was a last resort. They had tried everything else with varying degrees of success or failure. For example, at the time of her death--on January 19, 1956--Louise Carver could look back on a career which had embraced grand opera, the legitimate stage and vaudeville.

The film industry in the 'teens also boasted a number of nondescript comediennes, such as Victoria Forde or Minta Durfee, who has more claim to fame as Roscoe "Fatty" Arbuckle's first wife than as a comedienne in her own right. One such nonentity as a comedienne, Alice Lake, was to have later success as a star of non-comedy features in the early Twenties.

Billie Rhodes was, without a doubt, the most delightful of early screen comediennes; she exuded a charm generally lacking in stars of one-real comedies, and it is unfortunate that she was not allowed to appear in more features, and that those in which she did appear lacked good direction. If Mabel Normand was the silent screen's greatest slapstick comedienne, then Billie Rhodes was the equivalent in the

7

Alice Lake and Al Christie

field of "genteel" domestic comedy. One critic suggested
that a perfect title for a Billie Rhodes film would be "The
Springtime of Youth," because it fitted her personality so
completely.

Miss Rhodes entered films with the Kalem Company
in 1913 as a dramatic actress. She was spotted singing in
a nightclub by Al Christie, who, in 1915, put her under long-
term contract. In a 1920 pamphlet on The Elements of Screen
Comedy, Christie explained the philosophy of the structuring
of his one-reel comedies, a philosophy which was responsible
for the success of many of the Billie Rhodes comedies:
"While there may be a little exaggeration and a little stretch-
ing of plausibility, the situations and incidents must in a
general way be of the sort that might happen in real life to
real persons." After leaving Christie in the late 'teens,
Billie Rhodes appeared in a number of comedy shorts for

other producers, together with a half-dozen or so second-
rate features. She retired from the screen in 1924, and pre-
sently lives in Los Angeles.

A charming comedienne and a natural successor to
Billie Rhodes at Christie was Dorothy Devore. Born Alma
Inez Williams, Dorothy began her screen career with Eddie
Lyons and Lee Moran at Universal, but came into her own
under Al Christie's direction. (It is interesting to note how
good Christie's comedies from the 'teens appear to have
been, and how appallingly bad are his comedy shorts from
the late Twenties. It is also interesting to heed Christie's
eye for talent in those 'teens years; aside from Billie Rhodes
and Dorothy Devore, Christie also groomed Betty Compson
and Laura La Plante for stardom.) Know Thy Wife, released
on December 30, 1918, was one of Miss Devore's first Christie comedies, as it was Earl Rodney's, who came to Christie
from Ince. This one-reeler, in which Dorothy has to pre-
tend to be a boy rather than Rodney's girlfriend, is almost
a remake of a Billie Rhodes comedy of a few years earlier,
and illustrates Al Christie's fascination with having his players appear in "drag." (It is not surprising that Christie
should twice have filmed Charley's Aunt--in 1925 and 1930.
The farce seemed almost to have been written with Al Christie
in mind.) One can imagine the delight that Christie obtained
from directing two "men" clutched in a fond embrace.

Dorothy Devore became Christie's most popular star
in the early Twenties, until she left to go under contract to
Warner Bros.; she had made her feature debut in Charles
Ray's Forty-Five Minutes from Broadway in 1920. In 1924,
she appeared in Hold Your Breath, a feminist version of
Harold Lloyd's Safety Last, and I have often wondered if
Lloyd was perpetrating a small, private joke by naming the
department store in the latter film, De Vore.

A marriage, coupled with the coming of sound, persuaded Dorothy Devore to retire from the screen. She trav-
eled frequently, and even lived for a couple of years in Shang-
hai. For the last ten years of her life, Dorothy resided at
the Motion Picture Country House in Woodland Hills, California, and I had the pleasure of meeting her there on a number
of occasions. She was a petite, attractive woman with a
strength and a bravery which enabled her to teach herself to
speak again after a severe stroke. Dorothy Devore died on
September 10, 1976, at the age of seventy-seven, the last of
the ingenue comediennes, a breed which had truly disappeared

Dorothy Devore

with the coming of sound.

Fay Tincher began her screen career as a dramatic actress in 1914, with D. W. Griffith's The Battle of the Sexes, but soon progressed to comedies and became one of the Triangle Company's most popular comediennes in the mid-teens. She was famous for her black-and-white checkered costumes, which she wore because she considered herself too ordinary-looking, and as Griffith had pointed out, "She's just a plain black-and-white type, always photographs just as you see her, requires nothing but straight photography and is never guilty of producing strange effects on the screen." Actually, Fay Tincher was a fairly attractive woman, who might easily have starred in dramatic features. Miss Tincher came to Al Christie in 1919 to be his first star of two-reel comedies, with titles such as Dangerous Nan McGrew, Go West Young Woman and Rowdy Ann. Of the last, The Moving Picture World (June 7, 1919) wrote, "There isn't a dull moment in all its wild burlesque which develops from the fact that Fay Tincher is a wild Western Damsel, whom father sends to a fashionable Eastern seminary with a note saying, 'Inclosed find $1,000 and my daughter. Keep the $1,000, and return my daughter a lady. '" A fair indication of the subject matter of these comedies.

Today, Fay Tincher is best remembered for the series of Andy Gump comedies, in which she starred between 1923 and 1928, playing Min opposite Joe Murphy and later Slim Summerville in the title role. With the disappearance of the silent film, she also disappeared from the screen. I have found no record of her death, so one may hope that she is still with us somewhere.

Mr. and Mrs. Carter De Haven never had the appeal of their rivals in the field of domestic comedy, Mr. and Mrs. Sidney Drew, nor did they deserve to, for the Drews were definitely more polished performers. However, Carter and Flora De Haven had their following in the 'teens, and successfully starred in a series of two-reel comedies and an occasional feature, after a lengthy period in vaudeville and on the legitimate stage. Unlike Mrs. Drew, who was the "brains" behind the Drew comedies, there is no evidence that Mrs. De Haven contributed anything to a film aside from her performance. In an interview published in Motion Picture Classic (November 1919), she stated, "Our comedies are merely skeletons when we get them, and Carter fills in all the actions as we go along. Funny things just seem to

Fay Tincher

pop into his mind and keep us in a roar all the time."

The De Havens starred in a series of monthly Goldwyn releases, produced by Billie Rhodes' husband, "Smiling" Bill Parsons, during 1918 and 1919. In the autumn of 1919, they signed a contract to produce a series of two-reel comedies for Famous Players-Lasky. Flora De Haven's last screen appearance came in 1921 with a series of features produced by her husband. The couple were divorced in 1933, and Flora De Haven died in September 1950, at the age of sixty-seven. Carter De Haven is still with us, and some years ago he remarked to me, "I encouraged my daughter, Gloria De Haven, to go into show business. You know a funny thing. When Gloria was a little girl, they would point her out, and say, 'That's Carter De Haven's daughter.' Now they point to me, and say, 'That's Gloria De Haven's father.'"

Alice Howell is surely one of the most underrated of 'teens comediennes; her facial expressions and body movements are a delight to behold. An article in Photoplay (August 1917) explained, "They don't call it 'slavey' parts in cinema circles. They have a more inelegant name, viz: 'Slob Stuff.' It doesn't sound particularly classy to the finely trained ear, but it tells the story. Alice Howell is probably the most consistent player of these roles, which constitute a sort of feminine Chaplin characterization .... Her make-up is certainly the most grotesque of all the 'slob stuff' comediennes."

Born Alice Clark on May 5, 1889, she met her second husband, Dick Smith, while appearing in a De Wolf Hopper show, around 1910, and with him substituted for, and took the name of, a vaudeville act called Howell and Howell. Alice Howell joined Sennett in the early 'teens--her husband had worked for him earlier at Biograph--and one of her first important roles for him was in Tillie's Punctured Romance. In The Moving Picture World (March 2, 1918) she modestly described her entry into films: "I've been in show business about eleven years and there isn't really much to tell. I came to California because the health of one of my family [her husband] demanded it. Pictures claimed me because I had to earn a living. I've tried my best to make good. It was a pretty hard struggle for me to get along at first. When I started with Keystone there were times when rainy weather kept my salary down to as low as six and nine dollars a week. That wasn't very much to live on, was it? Thank goodness that period is over. I'm doing pretty well and I'm

Alice Howell

paid pretty well. That's all there is for me to say." Alice
Howell worked with both Chaplin and Arbuckle, and was particularly fond of the latter. Photographs of her out of make-
up reveal that Alice Howell was an attractive young woman.

From Sennett, Alice Howell went to L-KO, where she
really became a comedy star, to Century Comedies, and then
to Reelcraft, which she joined early in 1920. From Reelcraft she moved to Universal, before retiring from the screen
in the mid-Twenties. For Alice Howell, films were merely
a means to an end; she had invested in real estate, and after
her retirement, managed her various properties. Alice Howell's daughter, Yvonne, had a brief career in the Twenties
with Mack Sennett before marrying director George Stevens.
Alice Howell died in Los Angeles on April 11, 1961.

To end on a personal note, I featured one of Alice
Howell's comedies, Cinderella Cinders, released by Reelcraft in May of 1920, in a program at the Museum of Modern
Art in May of 1976. The audience response was extraordinary, with young film buffs declaring Alice Howell a major
screen rediscovery. Such enthusiasm more than endorsed
Stan Laurel's estimation of her as one of the ten greatest
comediennes of all time.

3. CHILD STARS OF THE 'TEENS

Long before the era of Judy Garland, Shirley Temple, Deanna Durbin, Freddie Bartholomew, Margaret O'Brien, or even Jackie Coogan, the American cinema boasted a regular school of child stars. Indeed, during the 'teens years, there were more children visible on our cinema screens than at any other period in film history, and the children the American film-going public saw were, almost without exception, not in their teens. There can be no question that these little stars were doted upon; the fan magazines of the era are full of interviews with two- or three-year-old stars who tell of their favorite doll or pet with a sickening regularity. When little Betty Marsh at the age of four received her first "mash note" from an adult admirer, the publicity department of the Triangle Company saw that it was immediately published in Photoplay, whereas they might have been better advised, perhaps, to inform the police of a potential child molester. But, if I might be allowed to write in the style of the period, the cinema was young, the world was young, the stars were young, and everywhere was innocence.

During the 'teens, the cinema provided an ideal employment situation for children. The laws which prevented children in many states from appearing on stage could easily be circumvented by the film studios. For many poor families in the Los Angeles area, a regular income was assured from the hiring out of their youngsters to the film industry. In 1915, any small child appearing on screen in a minor role received $3.50 a day. Grace Kingsley in the December 1915 issue of Photoplay devoted an entire article to the babies of filmland--or, as she described them, "these Tanguays of the teething-ring, these Barrymores of the bib, these Romeos of the rattle, these Sarah Bernhardts of the safety pin." She told of a mother weeping at the Griffith studios over the death of her baby. "One of the girls sought to comfort her. 'It might have been your husband,' she said, 'think, you still have him.' 'Ay, but the baby earned three dollars and

Olive Johnson

a half a day when it worked and never got drunk,' she retorted, 'and the old man only earns a dollar a day and drinks it up!' The baby was but six months old yet, though shown in but a few pictures, had earned enough to keep the family."

Each studio could boast its own child star, or, in many cases, its own group of child stars. The Thanhouser Company had under contract Harry Benham's eight-year-old son, Leland; Helen Badgley, "The Thanhouser Kidlet"; Marie Eline, "The Thanhouser Kid"; and Marion and Madeline Fairbanks, who began their screen careers as The Thanhouser Twins, soon became the Thanhouser-Mutual Twins, and by the Twenties were known as the Fairbanks Twins. According to Photoplay (February 1915), "Helen Badgley is only five years old, but is already the real prima donna of the studios, having more temperament than Emma Eames ever had." (For more information on the Thanhouser children, see "Marion and Madeline Fairbanks," by Jean Darnell in Photoplay [October 1913] and "Those Thanhouser Kids," in Photoplay [February 1915].)

The Essanay Company, not to be outdone, also had its own set of twins, Ida and Ella Mackenzie. The Company's most famous child star was Mary McAllister, described by Motion Picture Classic (October 1917) as "one of the most versatile and talented of child actresses," who portrayed the character of Sunshine Billy, and starred in a number of features for the Essanay Company's Perfection Pictures. Unlike most early child stars, Mary McAllister's career extended through the Twenties; she made her stage debut in Salt Lake City in 1920.

At the Edison Company, ten-year-old Joyce Fair was featured as Mary Jane in the 1914 series of Buster Brown comedies. Viola Dana, of course, was Edison's best known child star, coming to the Company in 1914 after her stage success in The Poor Little Rich Girl, as "Broadway's Youngest Star," and leaving in 1916 to join Metro, and to rise to greater heights of film fame. Yale Boss was one of the Edison boy players. Like so many of his contemporaries he faded into obscurity, only to reappear in the May 8, 1949 edition of the Los Angeles Herald-Examiner, in which his mother revealed he was now a fifty-year-old garage mechanic in Augusta, Georgia.

Phil Tannura, who was to become an important cameraman, began in the film industry as a child actor with the

Edison Company. He recalled, in an interview with the author on July 20, 1972, "I lived two blocks away from the Edison Company, and whenever they needed kids, why they'd come outside where we played right in front of the studio, and they'd pick us out. I'd no idea of being a cameraman, but I didn't like the acting because you'd take one scene a day, then you'd wait around doing nothing. As I looked around there, I found out the most interesting job was the cameraman's job. I inquired about it, and they gave me a job loading the camera magazines with film. Also, I was in charge of the cameras. As they brought the cameras in there, I'd take care of them, clean them up, and that's how I got my experience." Phil Tannura was featured in at least one Edison production, the 1913 Boy Wanted.

One of the first child stars to gain major recognition by critics and public alike was Mary Miles Minter, who, at the age of ten, starred in the Powers' production of The Nurse, released on January 22, 1912. It is as a young adult that one remembers her today, but it was in that film, playing under her real name of Juliet Shelby, that she made her screen debut, a debut brought about by her portrayal of the title role in the stage production of The Littlest Rebel, in which she out-acted her two leading men, William and Dustin Farnum.

Universal claimed to have the youngest child star in 1913 with Helene (Snookums) Rosson, a seven-and-a-half-month-old featured in Allan Dwan's Our Little Fairy, a half-reel comedy entirely devoted to exploiting Helene's charms. Claimed The Universal Weekly (September 13, 1913), "The novelty of the film is going to make it a genuine treat."

Another Universal child star was Billy Jacobs, featured in a series of one-reel comedies, acted entirely by children, produced by Universal's Sterling Company. The first film in the series, Kids, was directed by Robert Thornby, and released on June 15, 1914. In many respects these shorts, which also featured Olive Johnson (later with Reliance) and Violet Radcliff (later with Triangle-Fine Arts and Fox), bore a close resemblance to the later Hal Roach "Our Gang" comedies. By 1917, Billy Jacobs had become a Lasky child star, and claimed the distinction of having had Fannie Ward, Marie Doro and Blanche Sweet as his screen mothers.

Seven-year-old Matty Roubert was "The Universal Boy," featured in a series of one-reel IMP comedies beginning on July 16, 1914. In each short, Matty would meet a well-known personality, and among those who had the dubious honor of making Roubert's acquaintance were New York Giants manager John McGraw, Annette Kellerman, Oscar Hammerstein, Theodore Roosevelt, and Barney Oldfield. Matty Roubert had begun his screen career with the Vitagraph Company, and had also worked for Biograph before coming to Universal. Unlike most child stars his ambition in life was not to be an actor, but a director.

Also released by Universal were the Eclair films of Clara Horton, known in the early 'teens as "The Eclair Kid." Miss Horton, who began her career as an artist's model when still a baby, was featured in a series of "'Grown-Up' plays done entirely by children."* Among Miss Horton's colleagues at Universal were Baby Doris Baker and Zoe Du Rae, who later became better known as Zoe Rae. She portrayed Tiny Tim in My Little Boy (1917), a modernized version of Dickens' A Christmas Carol.

And there were still more children.... Gloria Joy of the Balboa Company was known as "the baby Nazimova." Edna Ross portrayed the young Helen Keller in the 1919 production of Deliverance. Ben Alexander delighted the female audiences in D. W. Griffith's Hearts of the World. Wesley Barry almost stole the acting honors from Mary Pickford in Daddy-Long-Legs. Madge Evans, whose screen career certainly did not end with child roles, gained her major screen successes with the World Company, appearing in, among others, Husband and Wife (1916), The Revolt (1916), The Little Duchess (1917), The Volunteer (1917), and The Little Patriot (1917). Magda Foy was the Solax Kid, and over at Reliance there were a host of forgotten child players, including May Giraca, Baby Kelcey, Edna Mae Wilson, and Chandler House. The last gave a memorable performance in the French Story of D. W. Griffith's Intolerance.

Carmen De Rue was born in 1910, and by 1918 claimed to have appeared in more than one hundred films. One cannot help but wonder how she found time in between screen roles to learn to count up to one hundred. Her father, Eugene, was an assistant director, who persuaded Cecil B.

---

* For more information, see "The Littlest Leading Lady," by Mabel Condon in Photoplay (November, 1914).

DeMille to cast her as Hal in the 1913 production of The Squaw Man.

On March 18, 1916, the Pathé Company released a five-reel Balboa production titled Little Mary Sunshine. It starred Henry King, who also directed, Marguerite Nichols, Andrew Arbuckle, and a child actress named Helen Marie Osborne, making her screen debut. Miss Osborne portrays a motherless child who wanders into the street and climbs into the automobile of a young man whose sweetheart has just left him because of his addiction to alcohol. Needless to say, as soon as little Miss Osborne displays fear at the smell of whiskey on the young man's breath, he turns over a new leaf. Baby Marie Osborne rapidly became a major star, earning three hundred dollars a week, and by 1918 even had her own film company. Then, like all child stars, she faded from public favor, which at least allowed her director, Henry King, to move on to better things. *

Catherine Reichert, better known to her fans as "Kittens," claimed to be the only six-year-old in the United States with her own name in the telephone directory. Born on March 3, 1911, she had played for many companies, including Famous Players, Ivan and Vitagraph, but it was as a Fox star that she became best known. She was not the most important of the Fox child stars, however, for she was easily eclipsed by Jane and Katherine Lee. Among other features, they appeared with Annette Kellerman in A Daughter of the Gods (1916), and by 1917 they were described as "the children best known to moving picture audiences."

Other children were to join the Lee sisters and "Kittens" Reichert at Fox, in particular Francis Carpenter and Virginia Lee Corbin, who were such a delight in Jack and the Beanstalk (1917). They are best remembered as one of the group of children at the Triangle-Fine Arts studios, a group which also included Charles Spofford, Georgie Stone (who also went to Fox), and Margie Guerin. Francis and Virginia are totally delightful in the first feature-length film to be directed by Sidney and Chester Franklin, Let Katie Do It, released on January 9, 1916. (The Franklins went on to

---

* For more information on Baby Marie Osborne, see "A Bear of a Baby!" by Allen Corlis in Photoplay (April 1917), and "Filmdom's Tiniest Star," by Roberta Courtlandt in Motion Picture Classic (September 1917).

direct Carpenter and Corbin and other child stars at Fox,
and their work has been documented by Kevin Brownlow in
"The Franklin Kid Pictures," published in the August-Septem-
ber 1972 issue of Films in Review.) The script, by D. W.
Griffith, has the children fighting off an attack on their home
by a group of murderous Mexicans, led by Walter Long.
None of the adult stars in Let Katie Do It, including Jane
Grey, Tully Marshall and Ralph Lewis, stood a chance against
such "cuteness."

Julian Johnson, writing in Photoplay (March 1916) sum-
med up the charm of Let Katie Do It very neatly: "Eugene
Field would have enjoyed this. He might have written it.
It is a big heroic of childhood, a nursery story about the
Trojan war, in which Ned becomes a little hero for some
Homeric lyre, and little Nellie a new Helen.... The comedy
takes on the proportions of an American Peter Pan."

One Triangle child actress, Betty Marsh, really deserves a paragraph to herself. The daughter of assistant
director George Bertholon, who worked with Griffith on The
Birth of a Nation and Intolerance, and the niece of actress
Mae Marsh, she made her screen debut as Blanche Sweet's
daughter in D. W. Griffith's 1914 production of Home Sweet
Home. She was featured in several Triangle productions,
including Enoch Arden (1915), Hoodoo Ann (1916), A Modern
Enoch Arden (1916), and Gypsy Joe (1916). Betty was an
adorable little actress, and most certainly worthy to use the
surname of one of the greatest of the screen's silent dramatic stars.

As an aside, it is worth recording that at one time
The Moving Picture World obviously considered publishing a
regular column, by W. Stephen Bush, titled "The Screen
Children's Gallery." Only two such pieces appeared--in the
March 28, 1914 and June 6, 1914 issues--and they were devoted to Yale Boss, Andy Clark and Edna Hamel of the Edison Company, and Audaine Stark, the star of the Ramo production, The Claws of Greed. W. Stephen Bush was obviously
very impressed by the last child: "One minute after the interview, Audaine was playing in the sunshine, bouncing her ball
vigorously. More than ever I thought then of Tintoretto's
head of a child."

If I were asked to name two child players from the
'teens whose performances most stand out, I would first
pick Thelma Salter's portrayal in the William S. Hart vehicle,

Betty Marsh

Bad Buck of Santa Ynez, released by Mutual on May 21, 1915.
The film contains a typical William S. Hart characterization, that of an outlaw, apparently totally evil, but who has
one spark of goodness in him, a spark which is ignited, in
this case, by a child, played by Thelma Salter.   "Tom Ince's
wonder child," as Miss Salter was called, was three feet,
six inches in height and weighed sixty-three pounds.   She
was born in Los Angeles in 1909, and began her screen
career with Majestic.   Thelma Salter also appeared with
Hart in The Disciple (1915), and was featured in a number
of Triangle productions, including The Sign of the Rose
(1915), The Crab (1917), and In Slumberland (1917).   Around
1918, she disappeared from the screen, but tried, unsuccess-
fully, for a comeback in the early Thirties.   She died on
November 17, 1953.

The stand-out emotional performance by a child was
by Lillian Read--the two-and-a-half-year-old daughter of
producer J. Parker Read Jr.--who to the best of my knowledge appeared in only one film, Thomas H. Ince's 1916
production of Civilization.   Her performance was perfectly
natural and very moving, and was, as Photoplay (November,
1916) noted, "the biggest bit of humanity in the whole pretentious spectacle."

Opposite: Thelma Salter as child actress in the 'teens and
in the Thirties.

Ethel Grandin

4. ETHEL GRANDIN

Many film personalities from the silent era show surprisingly little interest in their careers. Some of the most important silent stars--Alice Terry is an obvious example-- have no time for the past. Such is the case with Ethel Grandin, one of the screen's first leading ladies, who once commented to me of her films that "they were all alike, and I've forgotten them. They're in the back of me." Today, Ethel Grandin is a spritely and very beautiful lady in her early eighties, whose concern for the problems of others is at times deeply moving. Knowing her in the present, I cannot help but wish that I might have had the privilege of her acquaintance when she starred for Carl Laemmle and Thomas Ince. She may have been only an ingenue, but as those of her films which survive indicate, she was one of the best.

Ethel Grandin was born on March 3, 1894, in New York City. She has never shied away from admitting her age. Today, it's something of which she is proud, and as far back as a 1914 interview with Photoplay she commented, "I'm glad I'm just the age I am, and I don't ever intend to make believe I'm younger than I am." With her family's theatrical background--her uncle, Elma Grandin, was a famous leading man on Broadway, and her grandmother was an actress and dancer--it was no wonder that Ethel should have embarked on a stage career at the age of six, appearing with Joseph Jefferson in Rip Van Winkle. (Perhaps it is not amazing that people such as Lillian Gish, Blanche Sweet and Ethel Grandin are as energetic as they are today when one considers that almost their whole lives they have known nothing but work. It might be enjoyable work, but work nonetheless it was and is.)

For three years, Ethel played in Chauncey Olcott's company, along with Mary Pickford's sister, Lottie. During the 1909-1910 season, Ethel toured with Olcott in Ragged Robin. Mary Pickford had been in Chauncey Olcott's company as a veteran five-year-old actress, and when Ethel joined the company it was Mary's mother, Charlotte, who took particular care of her.

Mary Pickford entered films in 1909, and Ethel Grandin followed her a little under eighteen months later. Not surprisingly, Ethel's first choice for her screen debut was the American Biograph Company, where Mary had made her debut. Upon arriving at 11 East 14th Street with her mother, Ethel was met by D. W. Griffith, who promptly pulled up her dress and inspected her legs. When the young Miss Grandin became outraged, the director explained that he wanted to make sure she was not bow-legged, as were so many girls in the Biograph stock company. However, Ethel was so upset by Griffith's behavior that she refused to return to the studios, as requested, the next day.

It cannot have been coincidence that Ethel and her mother next approached Carl Laemmle's IMP Company, where Mary Pickford was currently working. She was seen by Thomas Ince, recently returned from directing Mary Pickford in Cuba, and was immediately signed to a contract. Ethel spent many months at IMP's 56th Street studio, working under the direction of Ince and Herbert Brenon, and once playing Mary Pickford's sister in The Toss of the Coin, released on August 31, 1911.

In the summer of 1911, Thomas Ince signed a contract with the New York Motion Picture Company to direct its production in California. It was the beginning of Ince's rise to fame, and to accompany him on that fateful trip to California he chose Ethel Grandin as his leading lady and Ray Smallwood to be his cameraman. Ethel and Ray Smallwood were to marry in 1912.* In California, Ince hired Anna Little, J.

---

* Ray Smallwood's career is deserving of a chapter to itself. He was a pioneer cameraman, who, as historian George Pratt has commented, with Thomas H. Ince "produced some of the best of the early Western films." Ray Smallwood was born on July 19, 1888. In 1918, he headed the camera department at Metro, and at that time The Moving Picture World (February 16, 1918) described him as "one of the most efficient practical men in the industry." He directed a number of features in the early Twenties, including The Best of Luck (1920), The Heart of a Child (1920), Madame Peacock (1920), Billions (1920), Camille (1921), My Old Kentucky Home (1922), Queen of the Moulin Rouge (continued on page 29)

Barney Sherry and George Gebhardt to swell his acting ranks. He also hired the Miller Bros. 101 Ranch Circus, with which he planned to produce "real" Westerns. The first such Western was the two-reel War on the Plains, released on February 23, 1912, and Ethel Grandin was its star.

Ethel Grandin in War on the Plains

The Moving Picture World of January 27, 1912 devoted a full page to commentary on War on the Plains, and noted, "It is a thrilling drama, portrayed amid natural surroundings

(1922), and When the Desert Calls (1922). He died at the Motion Picture Country Hospital on February 23, 1964.

by a capable company, and the photographic clearness is remarkable. Some of the scenes are sublime in their grandeur;
others are impressive in the number of people employed;
others are startling in realism and prolific in incident. While
there is plenty of action, the dramatic element has been well
sustained. Bravery and cowardice are sharply contrasted.
Love and jealousy play a part, but the impression that it all
leaves is that here we have looked upon a presentation of
Western life that is real and that is true to the life, and
that we would like to see it again and again so as to absorb
more of the details. "

Recalling "The Early Days at Kay Bee" in the March
1919 issue of Photoplay, Ince wrote, "One of the most exciting incidents of our early picture making was a grass fire
that nearly wiped out everything we had. The fire was caused
by a smoke pot igniting the grass and everyone, actresses
as well, turned to with water buckets, blankets and other
apparatus to fight the flames. I can visualize Ethel Grandin
made up as a bride attired in the once fashionable crinoline,
dashing madly about with her bridal veil wrapped about her
neck, taking frequent swipes at the fire with a wet blanket. "

One early Ethel Grandin production which has survived
is Blazing the Trail, released on April 15, 1912. Playing
opposite Ethel as Molly was Francis Ford, as Jack, and also
in the cast were J. Barney Sherry and Anna Little. In two
reels Blazing the Trail recounts an Indian attack on a lone
covered wagon, Ethel's being taken captive by the Indians,
and her rescue by Ford. There is a sophisticated use of
camera angles--at one point a herd of horses gallops between
the camera and the dramatic action--and the story, unlike
later Westerns, ends on a note of sadness, as Molly and
Jack visit the graves of those slain by the Indians. The
director, of course, was not credited, but Ethel believes it
was Ince, although she does point out that the action sequences
in many early Ince productions would often be directed by
others, in particular E. H. Allen. It is not surprising that
productions such as Blazing the Trail should have evoked a
three-page article, "The Bison-101 Headliners," by Louis
Reeves Harrison in The Moving Picture World of April 12,
1912.

Of the making of these early productions, Ethel Grandin recalls, "They'd build a set, and Tommy Ince would get
the locations, and you'd come in and do this and do that.
You'd rehearse one or two times. We never read a script.
He would tell us before each scene usually, and maybe once

Ethel Grandin in <u>Blazing the Trail</u>

in a while we'd know the idea of a story."

Carl Laemmle was impressed by the work of both Ethel and Ray Smallwood, and in 1913 he asked them to return to his company. His offer came at a propitious time; Ethel's mother was seriously ill in New York, and Ethel was expecting her first child. She recalls that Laemmle paid her during the three months prior to the birth of her son, and also for the first six weeks after the baby was born, a sure indication that Carl Laemmle was not only a kindly producer, but also that he didn't want to risk the loss of a star of the magnitude of Ethel Grandin.

There can be no question as to Ethel Grandin's popularity, or of her attractiveness. In a 1914 <u>Photoplay</u> article, Mabel Condon wrote, "She's as radiant a girl as you could hope to see. She has a wonderful skin, the kind that is described in excitable novels as 'ivory white with a touch of sea-shell pink.' And her eyes, also, are wonderful. They're a warm, bright brown that seems to radiate light, and the eyelashes are long and black. Then there's her hair, which adds even more to her beauty. It is dark brown and curls naturally, and Ethel just pins up the curls and her coiffure is perfect."

Back at Carl Laemmle's IMP Company, Ethel was starred chiefly in one- and two-reel comedies, a far cry from the Western dramas of Thomas Ince. Week after week, her films were released, including The Gold Mesh Bag, released on September 8, 1913; Love versus Love, on December 1, 1913; Love's Victory, on February 20, 1914; The Opal Ring, on March 5, 1914; Forgetting, on March 30, 1914; Where There's a Will There's a Way, on April 9, 1914; Beneath the Mask, on May 18, 1914; Papa's Darling, on June 22, 1914; and The Adventures of a Girl Reporter, on June 29, 1914.

She portrayed the title role in IMP's two-reel version of Jane Eyre, released on February 9, 1914, with Irving Cummings as Edward Rochester. As The Universal Weekly of February 7, 1914 commented, "Who is there more capable of interpreting the sympathetic, unfortunate little miss than the petite fascinating IMP star?"

Possibly Ethel Grandin's most famous role for Carl Laemmle, although at the time he knew nothing about it, was as Lorna Barton in George Loane Tucker's 1913 production of Traffic in Souls. The making of Traffic in Souls has been discussed many times--most recently by Robert C. Allen in Sight and Sound (Winter 1974/75)--and there is little point in repeating here how the film was produced secretly without Laemmle's permission.

Ethel recalls, "I was on salary, of course, but they hadn't worked out my schedule. I was waiting for my pictures to be written. George Loane Tucker saw me in the studio and said, 'Ethel, would you like to do a few scenes with us?' He said he had to finish very quickly. I didn't even read the story. I had no idea what it was about. I worked one day, skipped a couple of days, did another scene, and so forth. I thought I was doing a favor! It was very cheaply made, with canvas sets, so that when you closed a door, it would shake the set. I think it was the Daly Theatre in New York where they had a preview of it. They had a full house, and I was there with my husband. I was so excited. I hadn't been to one of these showings ever before, because I was just a little girl really. Everyone that knew me came up and congratulated me, and I thought, 'Why?' I didn't know I was in an exceptional film. I didn't realize it was so big."

In April of 1914, it was announced that "the Imp of the IMP Company," as Ethel Grandin was affectionately known, would appear in future exclusively under the direction of her husband, Ray Smallwood. (Smallwood, of course, had been one of her directors in the past.) It is not surprising that the idea gradually formed in the heads of star and director, husband and wife, that they might form their own company. Thus the Smallwood Film Corporation came into being, with a rented studio at Central Park West and Amsterdam Avenue in New York. Ethel remembers, "It was the top of a building, and it had been a Turkish bath. It had a really large stage, with dressing rooms downstairs, and a glass roof which let in a certain amount of light. We thought it was very nice." On December 21, 1914, United Film Service released the first independent Grandin film, a three-reeler titled The Adopted Daughter, in which Ethel played a dual role. It was followed, at weekly intervals, by Cupid Kicks a Goal, The Burglar and the Mouse and His Doll Wife.

Ethel Grandin's independent venture was short-lived. The reasons why are clouded in obscurity, but I suspect Ethel was happier taking care of her home and infant son than starring in films. Also, the age of the feature-length production had arrived, indeed had been with us for some time, yet the Smallwood Film Corporation was still producing shorts.

In 1915, the screen might have said farewell to Ethel Grandin forever. Thankfully, as far as her fans were concerned, it did not, for she made two highly successful returns.

The summer of 1916 saw Ethel at the Erbograph studios on New York's 135th Street, co-starring with Maurice Costello in the serial, The Crimson Stain Mystery. Miss Grandin enjoyed working on the serial with director T. Hayes Hunter; it was her first and only work in this field, and she enjoyed the shooting, much of which took place out-of-doors among the traffic and crowds of New York City, and she delighted in the daring escapades involving automobiles and fight scenes.

Ethel Grandin, the Imp of the IMP Company

The Crimson Stain Mystery involved a scientist whose experiments for good are turned to evil by one Pierre Le Rue, whose favorite occupation was apparently strangulation. It was released in sixteen two-reel weekly episodes, beginning on August 21, 1916, by the Consolidated Film Corporation. The episodes had such delightful titles as "The Brand of Satan" (the first episode), "The Infernal Feud," "The Tortured Soul," and "The Restless Spirit," and each episode was published in the New York Evening World. As The Moving Picture World (September 2, 1916) noted, "The Crimson Stain Mystery is made of the material that ensures the success of the serial film production, the chief essentials of which are the marvellous impossibilities that thrill the nerves and fire the imagination."

After The Crimson Stain Mystery it was back to a life of domesticity for Ethel Grandin. In 1919 it was announced that she was to return to Universal in a film to be titled Beyond Price, but nothing appears to have come of it. However, in 1921, she did return to the screen in two comedy features for S-L Productions: Garments of Truth, released on October 5, 1921, and The Hunch, released on November 28, 1921. In each film, Gareth Hughes was the leading man and George Baker was the director. One further feature followed in 1922, A Tailor-Made Man, a Charles Ray vehicle, directed by Joseph De Grasse, and released on October 15, 1922.

While still a major leading lady, Ethel Grandin decided to retire to a life as a mother and wife, a life which quite possibly brought her more personal happiness than she ever found in making films. But in her case domesticity's gain was quite definitely the screen's loss. What Thomas Ince had written in 1919 seems very pertinent: "Had she remained in the business I believe that Ethel today would be among the highest paid stars."

Even away from the screen, Ethel Grandin was not forgotten. Many would echo the words of Daniel Blum on the dedication page of his 1958 edition of Screen World: "To Ethel Grandin, one of my favorite silent screen stars, with affection and admiration."

5. FORGOTTEN EARLY DIRECTORS

The 1916 edition of the Motion Picture News Studio Directory lists more than two hundred directors active in the film industry at that time.   Of those, one or two, such as Tod Browning, Cecil B. DeMille, D. W. Griffith and Marshall Neilan, are still remembered today, but most have been forgotten by both the public and the film historians.   It is doubtful that anyone will ever be able to piece together the careers of, say, Charles E. Ashley, C. Rea Berger, Henry Clement Easton, Joseph Maddern, Louis Myll or Lester C. Tietjen. It is equally doubtful that anyone would find it a valuable or a worthwhile exercise to study the careers of any of these directors.   Certainly, only the resident historian of Colorado Springs, Colorado would care to examine the work of Otis B. Thayer, resident director of the Pike's Peak Photoplay Company located in that city.

It is not my intention to detail the careers of certain directors merely because they happen to have been directing for a period in the 'teens, but rather to examine the work of a small group of unfairly neglected men whose work was important to the overall development of the American film industry.   The men I have chosen to study in detail in this chapter, whose careers seem worth more than a passing reference, are Colin Campbell, J. Searle Dawley, Victor Heerman and Edward Sloman.

"A cold intellectual man" is how Lewis Jacobs described Colin Campbell, and he received two cold, intellectual paragraphs in Jacobs' The Rise of the American Film. He is not mentioned at all in Benjamin B. Hampton's History of the American Film Industry, Kevin Brownlow's The Parade's Gone By or Edward Wagenknecht's The Movies in the Age of Innocence.   Yet, in 1915, Colin Campbell was described by The Moving Picture World as "among the foremost directors in the making of photoplays in America. "   A year later, Photoplay (May 1916) described him as "a pace-maker

in the picture-telling of great dramatic picture stories." In
the 1921 edition of the Motion Picture Studio Directory, Campbell makes the proud boast that he had directed over five
hundred pictures.

So who was Colin Campbell? Little is known of his
family background except that he was born in Scotland circa
1866, the son of a Presbyterian minister. When or why he
came to the States is unknown. At the somewhat late age
of twenty-five, he apparently took up acting, and later became
a stage director for, among others, Edwin Thanhouser in
Milwaukee.

It would appear that in 1911 he joined the Selig Company as a director with the Los Angeles studio. The first
mention of his work at Selig appears in The Moving Picture
World of April 27, 1912: "Director Campbell, of the Selig
studio in Los Angeles, took a company over to Santa Catalina
Island April 1 for a ten-day stay. The scenarios which he
took with him were written to feature the marvellous swim-
ming abilities of Bessie Eyton." Colin Campbell was one of
three directors at work at the West Coast studios of Selig
at that time, the other two being Hobart Bosworth and Fred
Huntley.

The Selig Polyscope Company--to give it its full title--
was founded by Colonel William N. Selig in Chicago. In
1909, Colonel Selig was the first of the motion picture pioneers to embark steadily on film production in Los Angeles,
and by the time Colin Campbell joined his company, Selig
had a studio well established at the corner of Clifford and
Allessandro Streets in Glendale. Campbell remained with
Colonel Selig for some eight years, long after every other
member of the Selig Company had gone on to new pastures.
In fact, in the 1918 edition of the Motion Picture Studio Directory there is a half-page advertisement in which Campbell
proudly proclaimed, "Still with Selig." It is highly possible
that the two men stayed together for so long because they
both had the same old-fashioned attitude towards film-making,
with the story being all important and technique mattering
little.

At Selig, Colin Campbell specialized exclusively in
dramatic films. He was a director upon whom Selig was
totally reliant, as evidenced by the producer's assigning
Campbell to the direction of the Company's most important
production to date, The Spoilers.

The Selig Company's film of Rex Beach's popular 1906 novel, The Spoilers, was the first of some five versions, and it is considered by many to have been the most faithful to the original work. The film, however, has a greater claim to fame as one of the American cinema's first major feature-length productions, predating The Birth of a Nation, as it does, by some nine months or more.

The Spoilers

Making his screen debut in the role of Glenister was the eminent stage actor, William Farnum, who was later to become a popular leading man with the William Fox Company. The part was originally to have been played by Hobart Bosworth, but he left Selig to form his own company before shooting got underway. Of Farnum's performance, a reviewer in The Moving Picture World (April 11, 1914) wrote, "He is force personified." Kathlyn Williams, who had been a leading lady with the Selig Company since 1910, here proved herself to be one of the early screen's most capable actresses. Variety (April 17, 1914) thought it "doubtful if any actress could have improved upon the part" of Cherry Malotte. Also featured in The Spoilers were three leading members of the Selig stock company: Tom Santschi, Bessie Eyton and Wheeler Oakman.

The Spoilers was premiered at Chicago's Orchestra Hall on Wednesday, March 25, 1914, before some 2,000 people. It was subsequently chosen to open the new Strand Theatre in New York. The film was both a popular and a critical success; Variety commented that "To the rabid movie fan--the one who revels in action, excitement and panoramic succession of real life adventures--this picture hands him a wallop." So popular was The Spoilers that it was expanded from its original length of nine reels to some twelve reels for a reissue in February of 1916. This reissue featured footage, now lost, of Rex Beach at work in his study.

Campbell's direction of the climactic fight sequence between Glenister and McNamara (played by Tom Santschi) was well handled, and had an earthy, brutally raw feel to it that was missing from the later, more sophisticated Hollywood versions of The Spoilers, which boasted such names as Gary Cooper and William Boyd, John Wayne and Randolph Scott, and Jeff Chandler and Rory Calhoun in the roles of the protagonists. To The Moving Picture World, the fight "seems so real and so just that we whisper, between breaths, 'Amen.'"

What type of a director was Colin Campbell? The following word-picture by Harry Carr, published in the June 1915 issue of Photoplay, would appear to be fairly accurate: "Colin Campbell, who directed The Spoilers, is a keen, incisive, abrupt director. He has the admiration of his people and the bigger the people the more they admire him. He is polite, sharp, peremptory and effective. Mr. Campbell does not confide in the members of the cast. He knows exactly what he wants and delivers his orders with a precision that gets action. He depends very little upon the company to supply him inspirations. He is the intellect that shoots to the mark he has selected. As a director, Mr. Campbell strikes the observer as being cold, clear and intellectual." (There are those words again--cold and intellectual--indicating possibly that Lewis Jacobs is not as original in his interpretation as one might imagine.) Interestingly, there is a clue to Colin Campbell's character in a script for a proposed Selig production of The Lost World, in which the news editor of The Daily Gazette is described as "a typical literary Scotchman Colin Campbell type" [sic].

From The Spoilers, Colin Campbell went on to direct most of Selig's later major productions, including The Rosary (1915), The Ne'er Do Well (1915), The Crisis (1916) and Little Orphan Annie (1919). He left Selig in 1919, and was to become a director for the newly-formed Robertson-Cole Company which was responsible for a series of films with Sessue Hayakawa (The First Born, Black Roses and The Swamp, all 1921) and Pauline Frederick (The Lure of Jade, 1921, and Two Kinds of Women, 1922). During late 1922 and 1923, Campbell directed four features for Fox, starring Dustin Farnum, Three Who Paid, The Buster, Bucking the Barrier and The Grail, all released in 1923.

Colin Campbell's last two films were for an enterprise known as the Rellimeo Film Syndicate: Pagan Passions, with Wyndham Standing, and The Bowery Bishop, with Henry B. Walthall, both released in 1924. He died of a stroke at his Hollywood home on August 26, 1928. His death went almost unnoticed, with Motion Picture News devoting only one short paragraph to his passing.

J. Searle Dawley is perhaps a little better known than Colin Campbell. After all, he did direct D. W. Griffith in his first screen appearance, Mary Pickford in her second feature film, and one of the first sound-on-film productions. Yet for all these claims to fame, J. Searle Dawley is still a somewhat shadowy figure in the history of the cinema.

Jay Dawley was born in Del Norte, Colorado, on October 4, 1877. He made his stage debut, as a student, in the Lewis Morrison Faust Company, at the Grand Opera House on 8th Avenue and 23rd Street in New York on September 9, 1895. It was Morrison who told Dawley, "Jay Dawley is no name for the theatre. Change it, laddie, change it,"* and change it he did, adding his mother's maiden name, and using the initial "J." Dawley had moderate success in the theatre, and claimed to have written and produced eighteen plays over a five year period.

As a stage manager, one of Dawley's functions was to select the short films to be run between the acts of the play. As he recalled, "I went to an exchange conducted by P. L. Waters on 25th Street, between Broadway and Fourth Avenue,

---

*Quotes by J. Searle Dawley are taken from his notes in the Margaret Herrick Library of the Academy of Motion Picture Arts and Sciences, and from taped interviews with Howard Walls, recorded in November 1948, also in the Margaret Herrick Library.

New York.   Above this office, on the roof of the building,
the Edison picture company had a studio, over which was a
half skylight.   One day, while in Mr. Waters' office, I met
a Mr. Porter, who was in charge of the Edison picture company.   I was waiting for a reel to be run off and during the
wait, talked pictures with Mr. Porter.   I told him that it
was curious no company had gone in for stories with more
action.   I suggested Paul Revere's Ride, which would make
a good story, it seemed to me.   He was evidently interested
in both the suggestion and in me, for he investigated me and
my activities, finding I had been active on the stage as actor,
stage manager and playwright, that my mind was chiefly concerned with things dramatic.   What was my surprise to get
a telephone call from Mr. Porter one day asking me to have
luncheon with him!   The subject veered to pictures.   Porter
asked me if I would be interested in making them my pro-
fession.   I was doubtful.   Then he sprang his bolt.   If I
would come to the Edison Company as stage director, he
would give sixty dollars a week.   I accepted his proposition,
gave notice to the Spooners [a theatrical management], and
in two weeks was making one-reelers for Edison."

It was May 13, 1907 when Dawley joined the Edison
Company.   He was employed not by Thomas Edison, who had
little if anything to do with the film company which bore his
name, but by Edwin S. Porter, one of the true pioneers of
the cinema.   As Dawley recalled, "Bless his heart, Porter
was one great guy in the film business.   This great pioneer
was a quiet unassuming man with a delightful sense of humor,
a merry laugh and a penetrating insight into what the camera
could do.   Porter was cameraman, studio manager and story
writer."

J. Searle Dawley's first directorial effort for the
Edison Company was a one-reel (955-ft.) comedy titled The
Nine Lives of a Cat.   Somewhat jocosely, the director remembered, "I wished I had not picked such a temperamental
actress as a star.   She was beautiful, with lovely white
markings, white star on her forehead and long white paws.
But that was my fatal error.   The second day she deserted
us.   We had to get her counterpart and paint on the white
markings.   The paint didn't seem to agree with her stomach
and we had to send her to the hospital.   Our next cat looked
a lot like the original and we decided to take a chance.   Only
three days later she became a mother with five kittens--we
finally finished the picture, but I hardly thought I was going
to like the motion picture business."   Shooting began on The
Nine Lives of a Cat on May 28, 1907, and the film was com-

pleted, somewhat surprisingly, a considerable time later, on
July 8. Aside from the problem with the cats, another reason for the delay in completion of the film was that the first
actress portraying the wife, a Miss Levelle, suddenly walked
off the set and had to be replaced by a Miss Stewart.

One of the most important of Dawley's early films at
Edison, from today's viewpoint, was Rescued from an Eagle's
Nest, which introduced D. W. Griffith to motion pictures.
Edwin S. Porter is often erroneously credited with the direc-
tion of this film, but in fact he was the cameraman, while
Dawley was responsible for the direction. But, as Dawley
commented, "To be frank, it didn't need much directing....
To my mind, it was quite a terrible picture." Dawley's
opinion was shared by the reviewer on the staff of The Moving
Picture World, who wrote, in the issue of February 1, 1908,
"Rescued from an Eagle's Nest is a feeble attempt to secure
a trick film of a fine subject. The boldness of the conception
is marred by bad lighting and poor blending of outside photography with the studio work, which is too flat; and the trick
of the eagle and its wire wings is too evident to the audience,
while the fight between the man and the eagle is poor and
out of vision. The hill brow is not a precipice. We looked
for better things."

J. Searle Dawley remained with the Edison Company
until 1913. Among the films he directed were a series--in-
cluding Treasure Island, Napoleon at Saint Helena, The Relief
of Lucknow and Robert Emmett--shot on the island of Bermuda
late in 1911. Dawley directed a one-reel version of The
Battle of Trafalgar, released on September 22, 1911. Recalled Dawley, "I remember Mr. [Horace] Plimpton,* our
studio manager, was going away on a trip and would not be
in the studio during the making of this picture--Thank Heav-
ens--but his last order was, 'Dawley, don't have too much
blood showing. It isn't nice.'" A year later, in Cheyenne,
Wyoming, Dawley directed the first film to recreate The
Charge of the Light Brigade, starring Ben Wilson and Richard
Neill. For The Old Monk's Tale, released on February 15,
1913, Dawley hired a young man to play a bit part; his name
was Harold Lloyd.

---

* In an interview, on July 25, 1972, one-time Edison leading
lady, Viola Dana, told me, "Horace Plimpton didn't know the
first thing about pictures--He had been in the carpet busi-
ness--but he had to be called down before every take to make
suggestions."

J. Searle Dawley's The Battle of Trafalgar

On June 8, 1913, Dawley signed a contract with Adolph Zukor's Famous Players Company. Possibly Dawley's engagement with Famous Players was due not only to the ability he had displayed at Edison, but also to the fact that Edwin S. Porter, who had hired Dawley for Edison, was now "technical director" at Famous Players.

Dawley's first assignment with Famous Players was to direct the great stage actress, Minnie Maddern Fiske, in one of her most famous roles, that of Tess of the D'Urbervilles. It says much for the high esteem in which Dawley was held that he was asked to direct the film, for not only was he responsible for handling Mrs. Fiske, he was also responsible for bringing in a first-rate production. If the production did not meet Mrs. Fiske's approval, Adolph Zukor, the head of Famous Players, had assured the actress that the film would be destroyed.

Happily, Mrs. Fiske was pleased. For one thing, director Dawley had actually made her look young enough to be Tess! The critics, also, were pleased with the five-reel

Minnie Maddern Fiske in Tess of the D'Urbervilles

feature on its release on September 1, 1913. George Blaisdell in The Moving Picture World (September 13, 1913) commented, "Taken altogether--considering the story, the acting,
the direction, the backgrounds, the photography--Tess of the
D'Urbervilles is a great picture. Speaking calmly, the writer
believes it one of the greatest ever made."

Other stage stars made their debuts with Famous
Players in five-reel features directed by J. Searle Dawley.
Cecilia Loftus, supported by House Peters, starred in A
Lady of Quality, released on January 1, 1914. H. B. Warner
starred in The Lost Paradise, released on August 31, 1914.
Bertha Kalich starred in Marta of the Lowlands, released
on October 5, 1914. Of the last, exteriors for which were
photographed in Cuba, George Blaisdell in The Moving Picture World (October 17, 1914) wrote, "It is a worthy example
of the stature the motion picture has attained in the year
1914."

Late in 1913, Dawley directed John Barrymore in his
screen debut, as Beresford Cruger in the film version of
An American Citizen, made famous on the stage by Nat Good-
win. On its release, on January 10, 1914, The Moving Picture World (January 17, 1914) commented, "There is an abun-
dance of fine comedy as there are also many strong dramatic
situations in An American Citizen.... John Barrymore more
than makes good on the screen." Dawley enjoyed working
with Barrymore, and urged Adolph Zukor to put the actor
under long-term contract.

Most importantly, Dawley directed Mary Pickford.
Mary's first feature-length production had been A Good Little
Devil, in the stage play of which she had triumphed. Edwin
S. Porter had directed, but although the film was apparently
well received at the Third National Convention of the Moving
Picture Exhibitors' League on July 10, 1913, it was consi-
dered of too poor quality to be Mary Pickford's initial Famous
Players release. Instead, Dawley was assigned to direct
Mary Pickford in In the Bishop's Carriage, which appeared
on September 10, 1913, and is always listed as the star's
first feature. In the Bishop's Carriage was followed by
Caprice, again directed by Dawley and released on November
10, 1913. A Good Little Devil did not appear until March 1,
1914.

It is interesting to note that at this time J. Searle
Dawley was considered one of the screen's most important
directors. In a full-page interview in The Moving Picture
World of January 31, 1914, he discussed the art of the making of motion pictures. He commented, "Unless one appre-
ciates the beautiful things of life he cannot be a successful
director. The director must feel the atmosphere of a story
just as must the player. Do I plot out the business of the
characters in advance? Oh, no; I may not two seconds be-
forehand be aware what I am going to tell a player to do.
I simply let myself go and say, 'This is what the character
would do.' I try to feel for that instant what the person
would go through under those mental conditions. No, no
director can make every picture a success. One real good
picture in five is doing well."

In the summer of 1914, Dawley left Famous Players,
and with Frank L. Dyer, former president of the Edison
Company, and J. Parker Read, Jr. formed the Dyreda Art
Film Corporation, with studios on New York's 60th Street,
between Broadway and Eighth Avenue. Laura Sawyer, a
former actress with the Edison Company, was Dyreda's lead-

Mary Pickford in <u>In the Bishop's Carriage</u>

ing lady. Miss Sawyer starred in the first two productions of the new company: One of Millions, released on November 16, 1914, and In the Name of the Prince of Peace, released on December 7, 1914. Both films were anti-war, both were four reels in length, and both were released by World. For Dyreda, Dawley also directed the first screen version of A. E. W. Mason's Four Feathers, starring Howard Estabrook and Irene Warfield, released by Metro on May 24, 1915, and Always in the Way, released by Metro on June 21, 1915 and starring Mary Miles Minter. Of the last, based on a famous song by Charles K. Harris, The Moving Picture World (July 10, 1915) commented, "J. Searle Dawley, the producer, has lent his best efforts to the filming of the drama, in itself a sufficient guarantee that the work has been done in a thoroughly artistic manner."

Apparently Dyreda was not the success its principals had hoped it would be. Its studios were taken over by Metro, and Dawley returned to Famous Players. Here, Dawley embarked on the direction of a new star, Marguerite Clark. Marguerite's sister, Cora, who managed the actress's career, was impressed by Dawley, who between 1915 and 1918 was to direct Marguerite Clark in some seventeen features. The most famous of these were The Prince and the Pauper (1915), Snow White (1916), Bab's Diary (1917), and Uncle Tom's Cabin (1918). For the last, in which Miss Clark portrayed both Topsy and Little Eva, location scenes were shot near New Orleans, and it was here that she met her husband-to-be, H. Palmerson Williams. It is worth mentioning that Walt Disney saw Snow White while he was a young man living in Kansas City, and claimed to have based his cartoon character on Marguerite Clark.

Dawley was obviously very fond of Miss Clark. He recalled her as "sweet, gentle, lovely and kind. No director could have had a more lovelier [sic] star to work with. To her, motion pictures was a business as well as an art, and she never forgot that."

In 1918, J. Searle Dawley left Famous Players, by now better known as Paramount, to take a lengthy honeymoon with his bride, Grace, whom he married on June 14, 1918. He left with the title of "The Man Who Made Famous Players Famous." On his return from the honeymoon, Dawley became involved in the Sunlight Arc Company, of which he was vice-president. He also found time, during 1919, to direct a number of minor productions, including Twilight (De Luxe), Everybody's Business (W. H. Productions) and The Phantom Honey-

<u>moon</u> (Hallmark).

Fox offered Dawley a contract late in 1920, and for that company he directed Pearl White in two features, <u>A Virgin Paradise</u> and <u>Beyond Price,</u> both released in 19$\overline{21}$, and <u>Who Are My Parents</u>, with Roger Lytton and Peggy Shaw, released in 1922. From Fox, Dawley went on to direct three minor features, all released in 1923: <u>As a Man Lives</u>, with Robert Frazer and Gladys Hulette, for Achievement Films; <u>Has the World Gone Mad!</u>, with Robert Edeson and Hedda Hopper, for the Daniel Carson Goodman Corporation; and <u>Broadway Broke,</u> with Mary Carr and Percy Marmont, for Murray W. Garsson Productions.

1923 was an exciting year for J. Searle Dawley in that he directed three or possibly four films for sound-on-film pioneer, Dr. Lee De Forest. (Some ten years earlier, Dawley had been invited to take charge of the production of Edison's sound-on-disc releases.) The De Forest productions were photographed at the former Norma Talmadge studios on New York's East 48 Street, and included two episodes in the life of Abraham Lincoln, with Frank McGlynn portraying the President, and <u>Love's Old Sweet Song</u>, with Una Merkel, which was possibly the first sound-on-film story production. Dawley also recalled filming Adolph Zukor making a speech.

J. Searle Dawley's remembrances of Lee De Forest are well worth recording: "Dr. De Forest was a queer combination of genius and crab. Though he was a wealthy man at the time I knew him, yet at times he was quite a tightwad. I have known him to walk five blocks just in order to save twenty-five cents. He never seemed to conceive the great possibility of the things he had invented with the cooperation of Dr. [Theodore] Case [not to mention E. I. Sponable]. After we at the studio tried to convince him that to make anything out of his invention he'd have to go in for spending some real money on a big production--do things up to the standards of the day--but no, he never could be persuaded to take the chance. Then the Doctor said we could only use drops for scenery--scenery would vibrate and spoil the sound-- he was positive about that. One day when the Doctor was away we built a set of stage scenery and tried it out, and the results were excellent, and so another step was taken in the advancement in the art of sound pictures."

Somewhat appropriately, after leaving Dr. De Forest, Dawley became involved in radio in various capacities, including script-writing and office management. He retired in

J. Searle Dawley with Pearl White

1938.

J. Searle Dawley died at the Motion Picture Country House in Woodland Hills, California, on March 29, 1949. Various great names from the silent era, including Marshall Neilan and Sidney Olcott, attended his funeral. Mary Pickford read the eulogy, and director Walter Lang, who had once been Dawley's assistant, paid tribute: "We will all remember J. Searle for his warmth and graciousness and for his sincere desire to always help others."

Publicity-wise, most directors appear to have fared better than Victor Heerman. For one will look in vain for a mention of his name in any histories of the cinema or any film magazines from the 'teens. Yet his career spanned forty years and included direction of one of the Marx Brothers' most famous productions, Animal Crackers (1930), and an Academy Award for the screenplay of Little Women (1933), co-authored with his wife, Sarah Y. Mason.

Victor Heerman was born in the London suburb of Barnes on August 27, 1892. His parents, theatrical costumiers, emigrated to America and opened a business at 1566 Broadway, New York, on the site of which now stands the Palace Theatre. Victor was only nine years old when his father died, but even at that age it was necessary to undertake some work in order to help his mother pay for the upbringing of four children. Thus it was, in 1901, that Victor Heerman was taken by a neighbor to the first studios of the American Mutoscope and Biograph Company on Union Square, at 14th Street and Broadway. Victor recalls his first screen appearances:*

"The Company had some offices on the top floor, and on the roof they had a platform, I would say, probably twenty-five feet by thirty-five feet, and behind that was a smaller platform. These platforms were all on trolleys, like railroad things, so you could move them around into the sun.

"The first film I did, it was just a little box set. An old man was in a rocking chair, and I looked in the win-

---

* In a series of interviews with the author on May 17, 19, 24 and 26, 1976. The full transcript of these interviews is on deposit in the Margaret Herrick Library of the Academy of Motion Picture Arts and Sciences.

Victor Heerman

dow, and I saw he was asleep. His paper had dropped in
his lap. So I sneaked in, and tied a string to a fishpole
that happened to be over his head, and tied it to the rocking
chair. Then I took a paper bag, and ran around to the win-
dow, blowing it up. Then it went bang, he woke up, and
the fishpole would fall on his head. That was the picture!
I remember that one because I had to hurry around through
the back of the set, and I fell over a stage broom that was
holding up the door.

"The next one, I remember, I was to be a little boy
on a picnic with one of the girls, and we were to spread a
picnic, when all of a sudden a bear came, and we had to
run. And the bear turned out to be a boy. So the suit they
brought over from Christie's--that's the wardrobe, costume
place where they rented everything--why, the suit was too
small for the boy, so I was transferred to be the bear, and
he was part of the picnic. The picnic came in, then I came
around this tree, made a noise, and they looked at me, ran
away, and I came down and took off the hat, and was eating
all the things. But in the background, the woodsman came
in, with a big beard, and a hatchet over his shoulder. He
saw the head, picked me up, and the people said, 'What's
this?' So he leaned over and gave me some spanks, while
the others finished the picnic.

"Now the next picture I remember, because it came
back so many times in making comedies where they threw
pies. This was the front of a bakery--just a canvas painted
store, with a little hole cut in and a shelf here--and a man
is putting pastries out to cool. And this other boy--well, he
was practically a man--was a newspaper boy, and I was with
him. The fellow putting out the pies whistles over, and
says, 'What is it?' So the other boy shows him the paper,
and I'm to take the pies. I get the pie, but here's this man
in a uniform--either a policeman or a street cleaner--so I
give it to him. I told the other kid, 'Look,' so off we go.
The fellow who's selling the pies looks after us. He didn't
read all the news yet! Anyway, he says to the other fellow,
'This pie is mine.' They're arguing back and forth, and at
last he says, 'That is my pie; you give it to me.' And the
other fellow says, 'All right,' and bang, he gives it to him.
We had rehearsed this, and found the fellow was left-handed,
so we had to go back and change the whole set to do it that
way. Those are the things that you will remember. Of
course, in making old Keystone and L-KOs, why pies and
ice-cream cones went with the prop wagon."

Vivid as is Victor Heerman's memory of these films, he has no recollection of their titles, and a check in an extant 1902 Picture Catalogue issued by the American Mutoscope and Biograph Company reveals no films with these plots.

After his initial brush with the movies, Heerman became involved in the legitimate theatre, first as a child actor, and then later--around 1907--in a variety of capacities.

The cinema came back into Victor Heerman's young life in 1909 when he helped Edwin Thanhouser in the formation of the film company which bore his name (see Chapter 8). A year or two later, Heerman was hired by the Kinemacolor Company to manage its roadshow presentations. Theatres would book not only the Kinemacolor films, but also vaudeville acts in support. One such vaudeville act was Lillian Russell, who, when she discovered she was expected to play Scranton, Pennsylvania, and Albany, New York, commented, "Is that what the bookings are! I thought we were going to play cities," and promptly walked out.

Problems plagued Kinemacolor as far as Victor Heerman was concerned. He would speak to exhibitors and persuade them to book Kinemacolor subjects, only to find out that the Company was not producing sufficient films to fulfill the bookings. Eventually, Victor could take it no longer. "Looking at these Kinemacolor pictures every day! And nothing quite in focus," he recalls. "They were beautiful pictures and all that, but there was no expression."

Herman went to the Mutual Company, and "I saw these beautiful pictures, beautiful black-and-white pictures, with expressions in the eyes. I could never look at a Kinemacolor again." He was not yet producing films himself, but was put in charge of managing the theatres playing the D. W. Griffith features released through Mutual.

However, Victor decided he was getting nowhere as a theatre manager, and started looking elsewhere for employment. He recalls:

"At that time, we all lived at a place called the Bartholdi Inn, run by Polly Bartholdi, a marvelous woman who would take care of the actors. If they were a little behind, that was all right. She'd understand. Wally Beery, King Baggott, Del Henderson and other picture people lived there, and Ford Sterling, Henry Lehrman and Mack Sennett used to come in now and then. Sennett would cast his comedies at

the Bartholdi Inn.   Everyone who was not working would go
down to Coney Island and do a scene, and everybody got
$5.00, and that was all fine.   Well, the pictures turned out
fine, and they decided, 'We'll go to California,' and they
all did.

"Well, there was Ford Sterling, Fred Mace and half-
a-dozen of them that I used to lend fifty cents to.   Then
next year they'd come back with Stutz cars, and when Henry
Lehrman came back, he's living at the Astor Hotel!   I said,
'There must be money in them thar hills.'   So Henry was
getting his company together, and I said, 'Hey, Henry, how
about giving me a job?'   He said, 'I haven't got any money
for railroad fares, but you come out, and I'll give you a job.'
So I did.   I came out, found the Universal studio, and Lehrman showed up, and said, 'All right, you go to work.'"

Victor Heerman's first assignment in California was
as a cutter.   From that he graduated to title writing, and
then became a gagman.   When Lehrman became ill for a
six-month period, Heerman was given an opportunity not only
to direct but also to run the Lehrman company.   Shortly,
however, things soured for Heerman.   "Lehrman came back,
and I had just finished this picture, and he looked at it, and
said, 'It's fine.'   When I saw the film, the title came on,
'Directed by Henry Lehrman.'   I said, 'What the hell is
this?   You weren't even in the studio when I made this, and
you put your name on it.'   He said, 'You should be proud
that I'm willing to put my name on your picture.'   That was
the end!"   Lehrman ordered all his staff to work Sundays.
Heerman refused, and he was fired.

He was not out of work for long.   The films he had
been responsible for during his year or more with Lehrman
had not gone unnoticed.   Mack Sennett immediately offered
Heerman a job as a director.   Victor recalls that his first
Sennett film was For Sailors Only, but I can locate no information on a film of that title.   It is possible that the film
in question is She Loved a Sailor, starring Claire Anderson
and Jack "Shorty" Hamilton, and released on September 10,
1916.   One of Victor Heerman's most important films for
Sennett was Are Waitresses Safe?, released by Paramount
on November 18, 1917.   This two-reel comedy, starring
Louise Fazenda, Slim Summerville, Ben Turpin and Glen
Cavender, was described by The Moving Picture World (December 8, 1917) as "An extremely funny comic of the slapstick sort ....   The number is laughable all the way through."

Louise Fazenda, Tony O'Sullivan (in drag) and Ben Turpin in
Are Waitresses Safe?

Heerman's departure from Sennett came about in a
curious way. Sennett ordered Heerman to finish up a picture
on New Year's Eve. Angrily, Heerman recalls, "I said I
wanted every girl in the studio--Gloria Swanson, Phyllis
Haver, etc.--and Charlie Murray. Well, when I told them
all they were going to work that night, the squawk that went
up. I said, 'Don't tell it to me.' So I worked them until
about three o'clock in the morning, and gave them a call for
nine o'clock to go and make the chases. Murray comes in
half-boiled, and the girls were all put out, for it seems that
Sennett had a big house party with all the bankers waiting
for the girls, and I had kept all the girls working. He was
fit to be tied. He kicked up a fuss and began calling me
every name in the house. I said, 'That's it. Thank you,'
and walked out, and joined the navy."

On his return from the navy, Heerman settled down
to a long and prosperous career as a feature director, with

such films to his credit as My Boy (1921), Rupert of Hentzau (1923), Irish Luck (1925), and Ladies Must Dress (1927). Aside from the direction, Heerman was often also responsible for the story and/or screenplay. In the Thirties, he concentrated on scriptwriting, usually in association with his wife, Sarah Y. Mason, and his credits include Imitation of Life (1934), Magnificent Obsession (1935), Stella Dallas (1937), and Golden Boy (1939). In the early Forties he was forced into involuntary retirement through the efforts of Joseph Schenck, with whom Heerman had had a dispute years before. An examination of Victor Heerman's career reveals him to be a man with ideals, who would accept no nonsense from anyone. He was his own master, and, as such, could ensure a distinctive and personal style for all his films.

Recent years have seen something of a renaissance of interest in the career of Edward Sloman. Kevin Brownlow devoted an entire chapter in The Parade's Gone By to the director, and Patricia Erens published a study of his career with particular reference to the 1927 feature, Surrender, in the Winter 1975 issue of The Velvet Light Trap. However, neither piece paid much attention to Sloman's early work.

Like Victor Heerman, Edward Sloman was born in England--in 1885--but he came to the States much later in life, at the age of nineteen. He embarked on a theatrical career in 1909. "I was never the handsome leading man like so many of them were, so I always got the acting part of the piece," he recalled in an interview with the author on January 7, 1972. He appeared in many plays, including Parsifal, The Wolf, The Mummy, The Humming Bird, and The House Next Door. He appeared in vaudeville with Eva Tanguay, the "I Don't Care" Girl. "I was the stage manager. I played the head of John the Baptist for Eva's dance, and I also played with Eva in a sketch with my wife." However, when Sloman reached New York, he found that the United Booking Office, which controlled most theatres, and against which Eva Tanguay had fought, would not book him. A former character woman with the company, Lucille Ward, suggested Sloman come out to California to try and find work, which he did in the Spring of 1914.

Edward Sloman certainly found work fast. "The first part I ever played was the first day I arrived in Los Angeles. I was the lead opposite Cleo Madison. In fact I had to carry her up thirty steps, and make love to her on the way up. The Company was Universal, and the man who was directing

me, Wilfred Lucas, a year or two later became my actor
when I was directing."

Most contemporary sources indicate that Edward Sloman's first screen appearance was in The Severed Hand, a
three-reeler released on July 17, 1914. There is no evidence
that this was the film to which Sloman was referring, but
for the record, it was directed by Wilfred Lucas, and it did
star Cleo Madison. The Moving Picture World (July 18, 1914)
commented, "The story is rather ordinary, but manages to
get hold of the interest and keep it." An article in the August 29, 1914 issue of The Universal Weekly noted, "In his
first picture, The Severed Hand, Mr. Sloman distinguished
himself in the role of the Russian diplomat. He was then
cast as the personification of evil in Love Victorious, and
he acquitted himself in this task with great credit."

One of Edward Sloman's most important roles at Universal was as the villain in the serial, The Trey o' Hearts,
released in fifteen weekly episodes, beginning on August 11,
1914. Starring Cleo Madison and George Larkin, The Trey
o' Hearts was written by the popular--perhaps trashy might
be a more appropriate word--novelist, Louis Joseph Vance.
Sloman portrayed Seneca Trine, an old man of sixty-five,
representing "pure hate." As The Moving Picture World
(August 1, 1914) commented, "There is villainy personified
in the vindictive old paralytic."

Sloman recalls, "I was getting fifty dollars a week.
I had started at forty dollars. I was also writing stories
for which I received twenty-five dollars a reel, and my wife
was getting seven-fifty a day for working, so we were doing
all right. Later on, I knew I was the greatest actor in the
whole cast so I went to get another ten dollar raise, but
Isadore Bernstein, the manager at Universal, wouldn't give
it to me. So I quit!"

Around this same time--early 1915--Sloman remembered selling a story to Thomas H. Ince: "I was writing in the
small hours of the morning, and I tried to sell this story
to my director at Universal. He said, 'No, I don't want any
war stories.' So I sent it to Thomas Ince, and he asked me
to call on him at an apartment building he had on Franklin Avenue. He said, 'I liked your story. How much do you want
for it?' Like a fool, I said, 'Five hundred dollars.' He
said, 'Are you crazy? You know I only pay twenty-five
dollars a reel.' I said, 'I'm sorry,' and started out from
his office. He said, 'Wait a minute. If I don't buy it, what

are you going to do with it?' I said, 'I'm going to sell it
to Mr. Griffith.' He said, 'Come back here. Will you take
$450 for it?' I said, 'Yes.' That was the highest price he
ever paid for a story. Later, I found out that someone down
at Inceville made five pictures out of that one story."

Late in 1915, Edward Sloman was hired by Captain
Wilbert Melville as a director at the Lubin Company's West
Coast studios, across the bay from San Diego, at Coronado.
(The first Lubin West Coast studios had been at 4550 Pasadena
Avenue in Los Angeles. The Coronado studios opened on
September 24, 1915.) Sloman recalls he drove down to Coronado with an actor friend, and was introduced to Melville,
who asked him if he had ever directed a film. Sloman replied
that he had not, but he had directed many stage productions.
Melville told Sloman to watch him direct a scene. As Sloman
told me, "Melville turned to me and said, 'How would you
direct that?' So I said so-and-so-and-so-and-so. In those
days the actors didn't have a script; there was a little black
book that the director had. Right then the book-keeper came
and told the Captain he was wanted on the phone. He said,
'Go ahead, and direct that scene the way you told me it
should be.' So I did, and later on, around lunchtime, he
came on the stage, and said, 'What are you sitting around
for?' I said, 'What do you mean? It's lunchtime!' He
said, 'Have you directed that other scene?' I said, 'No.'
He said, 'Go ahead with the rest of them.' That's how I
became a director."

Edward Sloman's first production for Lubin was Saved
from the Harem, a four-reeler released on December 27,
1915. According to Sloman, it was the first film of that
length to be produced by Lubin. It starred Melvin Mayo,
Adda Gleason and L. C. Shumway. Sloman did not receive
directorial credit; that went to Wilbert Melville.

When Melville discovered his new director had also
been an actor, Sloman was made one of the Lubin Company's
leading men. The first Lubin film in which he both starred
and directed was Vengeance of the Oppressed, a three-reeler
released on January 6, 1916. Sloman portrayed Aaron the
Jew. Other films directed by Sloman for Lubin include Two
New Items, with Adda Gleason and L. C. Shumway, released
on January 24, 1916; The Embodied Thought, with Sloman
(as David Goodman), Hazel Neece and Adelaide Bronti, released on January 27, 1916; Sold to Satan, with Sloman (as
His Majesty Satan), L. C. Shumway and Ben Hopkins, released on February 10, 1916; and The Redemption of Helene,

with L. C. Shumway and George Routh, released on February 24, 1916. As can be seen by the close proximity of release dates for these films, Sloman was certainly kept busy; in addition, he was writing the occasional screenplay, such as The Dragoman, released on January 25, 1916. (The other writer at Lubin was a young boy named Julian Louis LaMothe. Sloman believed he did forty per cent of the writing, and La Mothe did the remainder.)

Siegmund "Pop" Lubin, founder of the Lubin Company, never visited the West Coast studios, but left everything under the control of Captain Melville. Melville would take the film which Sloman directed to Los Angeles for processing. On its return, Sloman would spend the evenings editing the film, and it would then be shipped to the Lubin headquarters in Philadelphia.

"I was working so damned hard, I went down from 160 pounds to 120 pounds," remembered Sloman. "So when Melville wanted to cut the lunch hour from an hour to a half-hour, I said, 'Nuts to you, I'm quitting,' and I quit. That was the first time I had an agent. The agent at one time had been an assistant director to Wilfred Lucas. He got me a job with the Flying A Company in Santa Barbara, where I did nothing but direct all the time."

Sloman signed with the American Flying A Company in February of 1917. On April 7, 1917, The Moving Picture World reported, "The old Lubin studios at Coronado are being wrecked and all the buildings razed except a large two-story adobe structure." It would appear that Sloman had quit Lubin just in time, or, perhaps, that without Sloman's directorial abilities, there was no point in Lubin's retaining its West Coast studios.

The three years which Edward Sloman spent at Santa Barbara with American Flying A he recalled as "the best three years of my life." He directed, among others, William Russell, Franklin Ritchie and Mary Miles Minter--the last in A Bit of Jade, Social Briars and The Ghost of Rosie Taylor, all released by Mutual in 1918. "She was lousy," he told me. "Very pretty, a beautiful girl, but a little son-of-a-bitch."

Sloman recalled one interesting experiment at Flying A: "You know all the night scenes in those days were done in the daytime. They'd tint 'em blue. So I didn't like that, and I had a scene where the leading man, Franklin Ritchie,

Edward Sloman with Joseph Schildkraut, star of <u>His People</u>

had to drive a car through a downtown street at night in a rain storm. I put a camera on a truck, and I put that in front of the car he was driving. On the other side I had another truck with two tanks, so they rained on him. That was the first time we ever did a scene that was shot at night in a rain storm."

While with Flying A, Sloman shot a serial, in which his wife was tied to a buoy floating off the Santa Barbara coast. He remembered the errie sound which that buoy gave off, and years later used it for dramatic effect in a Paramount feature which he directed in 1931, titled Murder by the Clock.

Edward Sloman quickly gained a reputation as a competent studio director, and among his later films were Shattered Idols (1922), His People (1925), Butterflies in the Rain (1926), Surrender (1927), Alias the Deacon (1928), Puttin' on the Ritz (1930), Wayward (1932), There's Always Tomorrow (1934), and A Dog of Flanders (1935). His last film was The Jury's Secret, released in 1938. He died at the Motion Picture Country House, where he had been a resident for a number of years, on September 29, 1972. One might have thought that in the 1970s there was more interest in film pioneers than in the 1920s, when Colin Campbell's passing at least warranted a paragraph in the trade papers. Such was not the case. No newspaper or periodical commented on the death of Edward Sloman. Like Campbell, Dawley and Heerman, he was a forgotten director.

Thomas Edison

6. MR. EDISON AND THE EDISON COMPANY

Thanks largely to the pioneering work of Gordon Hendricks, with his book The Edison Motion Picture Myth (University of California Press, 1961), it is now generally agreed
that Thomas Alva Edison was not the inventor of the motion
picture. It is also generally agreed that--except financially--
he was in no way directly involved with the film company
which bore his name. I side with the majority in both in-
stances--it would be stupid to do otherwise--but feel it necessary to bring to light one incident which demonstrates that
Edison was not entirely uninterested in the Edison Film Com-
pany--or to give it its correct title, the Edison Manufacturing
Company.*

By 1905, when the Edison studio was erected at 2826
Decatur Avenue and Olive Place, in Bedford Park, New York,
Thomas Edison's involvement in film-making was negligible.
As proof, if proof is needed, I would like to present com-
ments by two former Edison employees. First, cameraman
Phil Tannura, in an interview with this writer on July 20,
1972: "I don't think Edison ever came there [the studio] at
all. He had no interest in the picture business at all. All
he was interested in was recordings and electric lights.
Every year, all the company--the people in Orange, New
Jersey, and the people with the Edison Company in New
York--we'd hold a field day, and my job was to photograph
Thomas Edison every time he came to this thing. That's
the only time I ever saw the man." And Edison actress
Viola Dana, said in an interview on July 25, 1972: "Only
on the one occasion, I remember him coming to the studio.
I had the pleasure of meeting Thomas Edison that one time.
He was very hard of hearing, and I don't think he was vitally

---

* It is always delightful to note that early film companies had
no pretentions as to their products being works of art. Like
any factory, these companies were in the business of manufacturing a commodity, in this case films.

interested in the motion picture end, because he seemed kind of vague. I thought it was just great to be able to shake the hand of Thomas Edison."

The following reminiscence by J. Searle Dawley of why the one-reel Edison melodrama, Dashed to Death, came to be made indicates, however, a heretofore unknown example of Thomas Edison's interest in the motion picture. "Phone conversation--new auto to be sent over cliff in a head-on crash. Story to fit situation. New car sent for the job. Thought Edison had made a mistake, but decided to finish the job and then do the explaining and the excuses later. Made scene of auto over the cliff at Palisades, New Jersey. Success! Police want old wrecked car--glad to get it taken away. Back at studio--9pm call from Edison. Wants to know how picture made out. Started to explain. Edison said, 'Don't give a damn about picture. What about car?' Told him it was all wrecked up and burned up. Expected to get a call down, but Edison wanted to know where was the hind axle of the car--wanted the hind axle over at East Orange that night. So had to go over to Jersey, and find policeman I had given it to, and buy it back from him for $20.00, and send it over to Edison by taxi. Edison had been working on some new formula steel axle to see how it stood the strain and shock and fire. So that was why the melodrama Dashed to Death was made for Thomas A. Edison."

When Dashed to Death was released on August 27, 1909, The Moving Picture World (September 11, 1909) commented, "An Edison picture which makes one sit up and take notice when the automobile race begins, and when the Duke's machine plunges down a precipice, exploding and taking fire as it goes, enveloping its occupant in a blinding cloud of smoke and steam, the action is so natural that it seems as though the accident really occurred. The tangled mess of wreckage at the foot of the cliff which presumably contains the mangled body of the Duke is sufficiently realistic to satisfy the most exacting critic."

Not only did Thomas Edison find at least one use for the motion picture, in an age when films all too often boasted nothing more than action played out against a painted backdrop; he also, inadvertently, contributed towards the making of a realistic production.

7. KATHERINE ANNE PORTER AND THE MOVIES

A number of practitioners of other art forms--in particular literature--have, at one time or another, become involved with film. For some, such as novelist Malcolm Lowry, the cinema has been a profound influence on their lives; for others it has provided a source of income when needed, and nothing more. Possibly Katherine Anne Porter would fall into the second category. During a particularly low period of her life, motion pictures offered a steady income, but the author of Pale Horse, Pale Rider and Ship of Fools does not appear to have used her film experiences in relation to her writing, unless the cinema is to play a major role in the three pieces she plans to finish up before her death. Admittedly, in the short novel Hacienda, Ms. Porter does concern herself with a film company at work in Mexico, but the basis here is obviously the time she spent in Mexico, not the time she spent working with a film company.

Katherine Anne Porter has displayed all the traits of a movie star when it comes to discussing her life with biographers. John Edward Hardy in his monograph on Porter noted, "it is remarkable how few firmly established facts about her life are available," while George Hendrick in his biography, Katherine Anne Porter (Twayne Publishers, 1965), commented that the novelist "has been extremely reticent in revealing biographical information, expecially about her early years. "

Both biographers claim that Katherine Anne Porter came to Chicago in 1911, worked as an extra with a film company, and returned to her home state of Texas in 1914, after a bout with tuberculosis. In two conversations with Ms. Porter--in September of 1975--I learned a little more, but at the same time became more confused about her early life.

She certainly came to Chicago. "I was just coming out into the world and trying to find myself," she remembered.

"I was a very modern woman then .... I don't know why I decided to go to Chicago." In that city, she told me, she obtained a job as a reporter, at $15.00 a week, with the Chicago Tribune. Her first assignment was to write a story on the Essanay Company, which was headquartered in Chicago. Before visiting the studio, Ms. Porter saw her first film, which she remembers as Chaplin's Shanghaied; "the best picture he ever made as far as I am concerned," she remarked. Yet the two-reel Shanghaied was not released until October 4, 1915, long after Ms. Porter should have left Chicago, according to her biographers.

As Ms. Porter recalled for me, she arrived at the studios, which she described as "just an awful-looking place," and found two rows of people lined up before a large door. She was pushed into one of the lines, and moved along with it. Finally, a man, who was obviously the studio manager, pulled her out of the line and directed her to a dressing room, with planks serving as benches and make-up tables, and a pile of clothing in the center of the room. "You should have been as green of the world as I was," recalled Ms. Porter. "I had been elected to be an extra." She watched the girl next to her making-up, and then began to use the girl's lipstick. The young lady, whom Ms. Porter swears was Gloria Swanson, politely but firmly took it back, and suggested she bring her own make-up tomorrow. The assembled extras were called on stage to appear in a courtroom scene, and Ms. Porter received $5.00 for her day's work.

Remembers Ms. Porter, "I forgot all about having the job on the newspaper until five or six days later." When she did return to the Tribune, the editor told her she would never make a reporter, and promptly fired her.

Not entirely unhappily, Katherine Anne Porter returned to the Essanay Company, where she was to remain for six months. She recalls, "The Company raised me little by little, and by the time I was ready to go, I was making $12.00 a day." She was nicknamed "Little Blue Boy" at the studio, because she was one of the few girls there with short hair.

Katherine Anne Porter's film career ended when the studio manager called her in and told her she was to be sent to the Coast. She replied, "No, I don't want to be a movie actress." The studio manager responded, "Well, be a fool," and that, as Ms. Porter recalls, "was the end of my moving picture career."

However, Katherine Anne Porter was not quite through with the film industry. Quite by chance, I came across the following news item on page 1828 of the March 13, 1920 issue of The Moving Picture World: "The Arthur S. Kane Pictures Corporation announces the addition to its publicity staff of Katherine Anne Porter, a widely known magazine and newspaper writer who will be in charge of feature writing for the fan publications and newspapers." As Katherine Anne Porter was at that time, according to her biographers, "earning a living as a hack and ghostwriter," it is highly probable that the engagement with the minor production company of Arthur S. Kane was not her only involvement with writing on the motion picture.

In later years, Ms. Porter told me, she received three offers to come to Hollywood, but, as she states, "I knew I had no business out there." However, during World War Two, she claims--and I am sure she is correct--that she did accept a fourteen-week trial contract with M-G-M, and worked with producer Sidney Franklin on a projected film of Queen Elizabeth I's early years. She did not agree with Franklin's point of view when he wanted to leave out all the historical material, and despite a salary of $2,000 a week, decided to resign.

"It was just what I thought," she told me. "I was right to stay away. There wasn't one thing I saw there that was good for me." Columbia's 1965 film version of Ship of Fools would seem to prove her correct.

8. THE THANHOUSER COMPANY

Ragtime, the novel by E. L. Doctorow which has been described as one of the most important literary works of our time, begins in the city of New Rochelle, but today's readers of the book are probably unaware that New Rochelle had two other, earlier claims to fame. The first was that--in the words of the George M. Cohan song--it was "only forty-five minutes from Broadway," and, thus, a popular place for vaudevillians to live. The city's other claim to fame was as the site of the studios of the Thanhouser Company.

Thanhouser is not the best known of the early film companies. Few of its productions have survived, and they do little to gain the company a reputation for artistic achievement. Almost all of its players have long been forgotten, and only one of its directors, James Cruze, has any reputation, and that reputation is questionable, with only two of his later features--Beggar on Horseback (1925) and Old Ironsides (1926)--appearing worthy of unconditional praise.

So obscure is Thanhouser that there is even doubt as to the correct pronunciation of its name. Mignon Anderson, the sole surviving member of the Thanhouser Company, states emphatically that it was pronounced "Fanhouser," while Ethel Grandin, who roomed with Thanhouser star, Florence La Badie, claims it was pronounced "Tanhouser." What is not in question is the name of its founder, Edwin Thanhouser.

In 1909, Edwin Thanhouser was a veteran of twenty-five years in the theatre. For many years, he had successfully conducted his own stock company in Milwaukee, presenting a record number of 3,500 performances without closing his theatre. He was also the first theatre manager in America to produce Ibsen's Pillars of Society in English. Thanhouser's theatrical ventures had helped him amass a considerable amount of money, which he decided to invest in motion pictures.

At that time, Victor Heerman, who later became a highly successful screenwriter and director, was working with the Stock Producing Managers Association, and he recalls meeting the would-be film producer: "Along came Thanhouser, and he said, 'I'm going to make pictures, moving pictures.' I wasn't much interested, but he said, 'Do you know anybody?' I said, 'Yes, I know Griffith down at the Biograph,' because Griffith used to come by when he was trying to get actors, and he'd pay ten dollars, and you'd find a hungry actor for ten dollars. So we went down to the Biograph, and we got a cameraman there. The next thing was to find a place. Well we looked around and around, and at last we wound up in a skating rink in New Rochelle."*

The skating rink, which Thanhouser began converting into a studio in November of 1909, was located at Grove and Warren Streets and Crescent Avenue in New Rochelle, alongside the New York and New Haven railroad. Here Edwin Thanhouser began work on his first film, The Actor's Children, a one-reeler released on March 15, 1910, featuring two child actors, Orrilla Smith and Yale Boss. The Actor's Children was directed by either Barry O'Neil or Lloyd B. Carleton--Thanhouser's first contract directors--and was scripted by Mrs. Thanhouser's brother, Lloyd F. Lonergan, who was to remain with the company until his retirement in the summer of 1917.

Entering the film industry at this time as an independent, when the Patents Company had virtual control of production and distribution, Thanhouser was taking a considerable risk. But, as he recalled in The Moving Picture World of March 10, 1917, "I took a chance and boldly made nineteen copies of The Actor's Children without a single bona finde advance order and sent them out to nineteen dealers throughout the United States. Most of the exchanges were unprepared for the sudden responsibilities of buying a thousand-foot subject without thinking the matter over-several weeks. The result was that, of the nineteen copies sent out, ten were returned, most of them with letters saying that they were agreeably surprised at the interesting production we had turned out, and if we expected to make another one to be sure and let them see it, as they would enjoy looking at it."

---

* In an interview with the author, May 17, 1976.

The Early Life of David Copperfield, released on
October 17, 1911

Thanhouser's second production, St. Elmo, based on
the popular novel by Augusta Jane Evans, and released on
March 24, 1910, was more successful. It featured the company's first leading man, Frank Crane, who left in July of
1911 to become a director with the short-lived Comet Company.

In its first two years of life, the Thanhouser Company
built up a stock company of players, including Florence La
Badie, Marguerite Snow, Mignon Anderson, James Cruze,
William Russell, Morris Foster, Harry Benham and Riley
Chamberlin. Several child players were also put under con-

tract: Helen Badgley (The Thanhouser Kidlet), Marie Eline
(The Thanhouser Kid), and Marion and Madeline Fairbanks
(The Thanhouser Twins). Thanhouser also boasted a black
actor named Nicholas Jordan, who made his screen debut in
The Actor's Children, but, as The Moving Picture World of
September 10, 1910 noted, "It must be mentioned that 'Nick,'
as the colored comedian is familiarly known, is only an occasional member of the Thanhouser players--in fact, plays
with them merely when he isn't busy at his larger, higher
task. This is the gentle art of keeping the Thanhouser floors
bright and shining and the Thanhouser ceilings free of all
cobwebs."

     Among Thanhouser's better known one- and two-reelers
from 1911 and 1912 were: The Last of the Mohicans, released on November 10, 1911; She, released on December 26,
1911; Dr. Jekyll and Mr. Hyde, released on January 16, 1912;
The Cry of the Children, released on April 30, 1912; Jess,
released on May 21, 1912; Under Two Flags, released on
July 7, 1912; and The Merchant of Venice, released on July
26, 1912. It should be noted that Thanhouser produced many
films based on the novels of H. Rider Haggard. Reviewing
its adaptation of She, previously filmed by Edison two years
earlier, W. Stephen Bush wrote in The Moving Picture World
(December 23, 1911), "In the present production they have
succeeded in making a mysterious novel very plain to the
average moving picture patron, and in so doing they have at
the same time kept up their high standard of art and dignity
in rendering this strange piece of fiction into moving pictures."

     In January of 1912, Thanhouser opened a winter studio
in Jacksonville, Florida. The Company enjoying the Florida
sunshine consisted of Marguerite Snow, Florence La Badie,
Viola Alberta, James Cruze, William Russell, Joseph Gray-
bill, Lucy Tanguay, Violet Gooding, Helena Whitely, Edward
Norton, Frank O'Neill, and Frederick Doering. George Nichols was the resident director, with Calvin Dix as stage manager and A. H. Moses, Jr. as the cameraman. The first
Florida release--on March 1, 1912--was The Arab's Bride.

     In many ways, 1912 was an eventful year for the Com-
pany. In April it was announced that Thanhouser had been
acquired by a syndicate headed by C. J. Hite. In July, in-
corporation papers were filed, naming Hite, Crawford Livingston, and Wilbert Shallenberger as owners of the Company.
Edwin Thanhouser agreed to stay on as general manager until
the end of the year, at which time he retired.

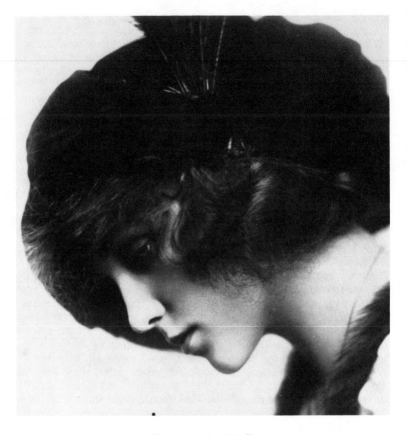

Florence La Badie

Charles J. Hite, an Ohio-born business man in his early thirties, had entered the film industry in Chicago in 1906, with his own film exchange. He then formed the H & H Film Service Company with Samuel Hutchinson, who was to head the American Film Manufacturing Company, and who afterwards began the Majestic Film Exchange. Later, Hite was to become the vice-president of Mutual.

The Thanhouser Company began to expand rapidly. In June 1912 it started releasing a two-reel feature every week, and in December of the same year, sent its first company, headed by actress Florence La Badie and director Lucius Henderson, to California. When the Thanhouser's Cali-

fornia Company returned to New Rochelle in April of 1913,
its Los Angeles studio was taken over by Mutual. On September 13, 1912, Thanhouser released The Birth of the Lotus
Blossom, the first in a series produced by its Japanese stock
company, headed by Taku Takagi. The series was intended
to present "real depictions of real Japanese life, by real
Japanese photoplayers."

The year 1913 began dramatically for the Thanhouser
Company. At 1:30 p.m. on January 13, the studios were
destroyed by a fire which began in the film perforating room
and quickly spread through the two-story structure. Tem-
porary studios were located at Main Street and Echo Avenue,
New Rochelle, and by the end of March, Thanhouser was
back in full operation, with four large stages under the all-
glass roof, and two open-air stages for summer use.

The resulting publicity from the fire persuaded the
Company to release--on February 4, 1913--When the Studio
Burned, described as "the last word in Thanhouser enterprise." Written by Lloyd F. Lonergan, directed by Lawrence
Marston, and featuring Marguerite Snow, James Cruze, and
the Thanhouser Kidlet, its climax was a studio fire, but,
contrary to what many historians have written, it did not
include any footage of the actual Thanhouser studio fire.

On June 14, 1913, Thanhouser announced that the noted
stage actress, Maude Fealy, was to become a member of
its stock company. She was featured in a series of lavish
productions, beginning with Moths, based on the novel by
Ouida, and including King Rene's Daughter, Frou Frou, Little
Dorrit and Pamela Congreve.

Thanhouser entered the serial field in 1914 with The
Million Dollar Mystery, starring Florence La Badie, James
Cruze and Marguerite Snow, and directed by a newcomer to
the Thanhouser ranks, Howell Hansell. Produced at a cost
of $80,000, it was claimed the serial grossed $1,600,000.
Interestingly, the financing and distribution of The Million
Dollar Mystery was handled by W. Ray Johnson, who had
been C. J. Hite's secretary. Johnson, in 1935, became
president of Republic Pictures, but withdrew a year later
to accept the position of president of Monogram.

The Million Dollar Mystery was followed by Zudora,
which was not a success. The Loew circuit canceled the
serial after the first five episodes because of the poor quality of the production. A sophisticated audience of today view-

Maude Fealy and William Russell in <u>Little Dorrit</u>, released
on July 29, 1913

ing a chapter of Zudora is completely confused by the incom-
prehensible plot, and one is hard pressed to understand how
Thanhouser would dare to produce, let alone release, such
a monstrosity.

On August 22, 1914, Charles J. Hite died as a result
of an automobile accident the previous day. His death left
the Thanhouser Company in a sound financial position, but
without a production head. It therefore came as no surprise
when, on February 22, 1915, Edwin Thanhouser returned to
the company which bore his name, in the capacity of president. Reported Photoplay (May, 1915), "Edwin Thanhouser
walked into his office in New Rochelle and resumed general
charge of his company; at the same time his wife, with a
'Good morning!' which might have been merely a pleasant
salutation after a night's absence, resumed her own desk--
which has apparently been kept as a melancholy memento of
an energetic and thoroughly feminine woman--and her own
method of scenario revision and dramatic 'snapping up.'"
The Moving Picture World (March 6, 1915) commented, "It
is pleasant to record the return to the manufacturing fold of
this veteran of the film industry and of the theatrical world
as well. We may be sure he will make his presence felt,
and for the good of pictures as a whole."

Like most early film companies, Thanhouser did not
limit its filming to its home studios. In August of 1913, a
party of Thanhouser players, including Florence La Badie
and William Russell, might be found producing a series of
seashore stories at Cape May, New Jersey. And in the
autumn of 1914, Mignon Anderson and Morris Foster, who
were to marry in April of the following year, headed a company of Thanhouser players shooting on location in Yellow-
stone National Park--the first group of actors granted permission to film there.

December 16, 1915 saw the release of a five-reel
Thanhouser production based on George Eliot's novel, The
Mill on the Floss, with Mignon Anderson in the leading role.
Directed by Eugene Moore, who had worked for Edwin Thanhouser in his Milwaukee stock company, and who also played
the head of the Tulliver family in the film, The Mill on the
Floss was typical of Thanhouser productions of the period--
dull and lacking dramatic impact. Even the flood sequence
at the film's climax has no excitement, thanks to staid direction and static camerawork. One pleasant aspect of the
production was Mignon Anderson, and one can entirely agree
with Margaret I. MacDonald, who wrote in The Moving Pic-

Mignon Anderson

ture World (December 18, 1915), "Mignon Anderson as Maggie Tulliver is especially pleasing. She gives an apparently effortless portrayal of the impulsive character of the miller's daughter, and is never more attractive than when in open rebellion against the application of curl papers to her naturally straight hair. Or when in an angry fret she pushes her curly headed cousin Lucy, dressed in all her finery, into the water."

Drastic reorganization of the Thanhouser Company was undertaken in the spring of 1916. All short film production ceased, and the June 2, 1916 issue of Variety announced that seven directors, seven cameramen and thirty-five actors were being let go by the Company. A contract was signed with Pathé, whereby Thanhouser would produce two five-reel features every month for release through Pathé's Gold Rooster program. Sixty-five per cent of the profits were to go to Thanhouser, and the remaining thirty-five per cent to Pathé.

The first Thanhouser feature to be released--on August 14, 1916--under the new agreement was The Fugitive, directed by Frederick Sullivan. There were occasional problems; Pathé refused to release King Lear, featuring Frederick Warde, because it was a costume picture. Two Thanhouser films which Pathé did release were those in which Jeanne Eagels made her screen debut: The World and the Woman, directed by Eugene Moore and released on November 19, 1916, and Fires of Youth, directed by Emile Chautard and released on June 17, 1917. Neither production was particularly outstanding, and neither did anything to advance Miss Eagels' career.

1917 was a sad year for Thanhouser. On January 24, Riley Chamberlin, who had acted with the Thanhouser Company for five years and with the Thanhouser stage company in Milwaukee for seven, died at the age of sixty-two. On October 13, Florence La Badie, the Company's most popular star, died from injuries she had received in a car accident two months earlier. Like Chamberlin, she had been with Thanhouser for five years.

On September 21, 1917, Variety reported that Edwin Thanhouser was planning to retire, and that "The Thanhouser studio at New Rochelle is practically idle now, with no-one there except the bookkeeper and Mr. Thanhouser."

On February 2, 1918, Edwin Thanhouser left the Company for a second and final time, retiring to his estate at

Bayville, Long Island. Crawford Livingston was elected president of the Company, with Wilbert Shallenberger, who was at that time president of the Arrow Film Corporation, in charge of production. No productions were actually announced, and the studio was loaned out to Clara Kimball Young.

Then, on April 22, 1919, The New York Dramatic Mirror announced the sale of the studio to Shallenberger and Crawford. Their ownership of the property was short-lived. In August of the same year, it was acquired by A. H. Fischer, who renamed it Fischer Studios and announced that it would be the home of B. A. Rolfe Productions, which released through Metro. "Thus," noted Exhibitor's Trade Review (August 30, 1919), "passes from film history a name that was identified with motion pictures since the days of the single reeler."

Edwin Thanhouser died at his New York home on March 2, 1956, at the age of ninety. With so few Thanhouser productions surviving, all that is left to record the Company's existence are articles and news items in trade papers of the day. To paraphrase a Moving Picture World reporter, writing of Thanhouser productions in 1912, these articles and news items "appear now and then like brilliant little torches to light our way in the evolution of this fascinating art."

9. THE PARALTA COMPANY

Little as may be the notice afforded film companies
from the early 'teens, it is more than many short-lived
companies from the later 'teens have received. Few historians have displayed even passing interest in the Paralta
Company, yet during its one year of existence it boasted a
number of major stars, including Henry B. Walthall, J.
Warren Kerrigan, Bessie Barriscale and Louise Glaum,
under contract, not to mention five directors of very differ-
ing skills: the artistically inclined Rex Ingram, the com-
mercially successful Wallace Worsley, the pioneer Oscar
Apfel, and the former Ince contract directors, Raymond B.
West and Reginald Barker.

Paralta Plays, Inc. officially came into being on
March 22, 1917, with Carl Anderson as president, Herman
Katz as treasurer, and Robert T. Kane as vice-president.
Nat L. Brown was secretary and general manager, and
Herman Fichtenberg chairman of the board of directors.
Anderson had previously been involved with the Lasky Com-
pany, while Fichtenberg owned a chain of motion picture
theatres in New Orleans. Robert T. Kane was named head
of production, and the new company opened its first offices
at 729 Seventh Avenue in New York City.

When Paralta was formed, it was announced that its
main purpose was to give the exhibitor a fair deal. How
this was to be done was explained in an article in the April
14, 1917 issue of Motion Picture News. The important point
was that the exhibitor would acquire a film not for a week or
a split-week, but for a whole year. The exhibitor had the
exclusive right to a Paralta production in his territory for
a full twelve months, and could screen it as many times as
he wished during that period. "Buy for the year; not for
the day," was the Paralta slogan. "Do not rent feature films,
but buy them for a territory for a specific time." The Paralta plan was explained to Southern and Western exhibitors on

April 26, 1917 by Carl Anderson, and to Northwestern exhibitors on May 3, 1917.

There is a certain similarity between Paralta's idea and that of First National, which came into being at approximately the same time. Both were inspired by the idea of working for the benefit of the exhibitors, and both were the brainchild of persons from the exhibiting field.

On June 30, 1917, Paralta signed a contract with Triangle for the distribution of its product, but the contract was terminated three months later, before the release of a single film. The contract had originally come about because of the close friendship between Carl Anderson and Stephen A. Lynch of Triangle. When Lynch decided to sell his interest in Triangle, Anderson terminated the agreement.

In the meantime, Motion Picture News on May 12, 1917 announced that Robert T. Kane had taken up residence in Los Angeles to supervise the first two Paralta productions, which were "going forward very rapidly." Much indeed was happening at Paralta's Los Angeles studios. Seven stars were under contract: Bessie Barriscale, J. Warren Kerrigan, Henry B. Walthall, Rhea Mitchell, Howard Hickman, Clara Williams, and Lois Wilson. Supporting actors under contract to Paralta included Eugene Pallette, Edward Coxen and Wallace Worsley, who was soon to try his hand at directing. Among the "bit" players at the studio were stars-to-be Leatrice Joy and John Gilbert. In an advertisement in The Moving Picture World of October 6, 1917, Paralta announced that it had arranged to film the works of a number of well-known American authors, including Mrs. Wilson Woodrow and Rupert Hughes. R. Holmes Paul was art director; David M. Hartford was casting director; and Clyde De Vinna, Guy L. Wilky and Robert Newhart comprised the camera force at Paralta. Robert Brunton, formerly general art director for Ince, was named production manager.

The bulk of Paralta personnel were former Ince employees. Bessie Barriscale, her husband Howard Hickman, and Clara Williams had all been Ince stars. Monte Katterjohn, who headed Paralta's scenario department, had held a similar position with Ince. Two Paralta directors, Reginald Barker and Raymond B. West, had both been prominent at the Ince studios. West's appointment was a major coup for Paralta; he had been responsible for the most famous of Thomas H. Ince productions, Civilization. It was perhaps

Reginald Barker

the lack of credit he received for his work on Civilization
that persuaded West to join Paralta. The Moving Picture
World of October 6, 1917 noted, "The engagement of Mr.
West marks an important step in the determination of Mr.
Anderson, president of Paralta, and Robert T. Kane, vice-
president, to retain the services of a battery of directors,
who, in talent, versatility, experience and reputation, will
enjoy the entire confidence of exhibitors throughout the country. In annexing Mr. West, Reginald Barker and Oscar
Apfel, they have undoubtedly attained their purpose." As
a Paralta press release described West, he was "an ardent
disciple of Thomas Ince, outgrowing his environs--his genius
surely outdistancing even his former master. One of the
fourteen really great directors of motion pictures."

Filming on the first Paralta production, A Man's Man,
starring Warren J. Kerrigan, and directed by Oscar Apfel,
got under way on June 4, 1917. A year from that date, it
was announced, Paralta would have fifty-two all-star features
ready, which would live up to Paralta's trade-mark of "Pick

of the Pictures."

Despite all the activity, no films were actually released until January of 1918, when Paralta began offering
its product to distributors, initially through the General Film
Service, and later through Hodkinson. A Man's Man was one
of the first to be released, closely followed by Madame Who,
starring Bessie Barriscale and Howard Hickman, and directed
by Reginald Barker.

Few Paralta productions appear to have survived,
which is unfortunate, particularly in Bessie Barriscale's
case, because she was an extremely talented actress, with
a hauntingly beautiful face. She starred in Raymond B. West's
first Paralta production, Within the Cup, which was advertised as "one of the most pretentious presentations attempted
during the past year. It has cost as much as five features
of West's early days and is expected to make ten times as
much money." Of Bessie Barriscale's Madame Who, The
Moving Picture World (January 5, 1918) commented, "This
seven-reel offering must be added to the list of successful
Civil War stories. Adapted by Monte M. Katterjohn from a
narrative by Harold McGrath, it contains plenty of plot and
action, as might be expected. In addition, the number has
been given very careful attention in the matter of settings,
costuming, characterizations and the further details that make
for an atmosphere in keeping with the times depicted."

Another early Paralta release was Carmen of the
Klondike, which has survived, albeit in an incomplete form,
starring Clara Williams, and directed by Reginald Barker.
Henry B. Walthall began shooting his films for Paralta at
the beginning of 1918, and to direct him the Company signed
Rex Ingram, who had previously been with Universal. The
first Ingram/Walthall production was His Robe of Honor, based
on a book by Ethel and James Dorrance which dealt with
political intrigue, in which the star was supported by his wife
Mary Charleson and Lois Wilson. Reviews were moderately
favorable, although most critics found faults. Edward Weitzel
in The Moving Picture World (February 2, 1918) commented,
"Rex Ingram directed the picture. Most of his work is well
done, but he has made two noticeable errors. One is in
using an office boy as the guardian of some safe deposit
vaults; the other is a mistake in the location of the characters
during the courtroom scenes." Walthall and Ingram quickly
followed His Robe of Honor with Humdrum Brown, and then
Rex Ingram moved on to Metro and to greater fame and fortune.

Bessie Barriscale

Bessie Barriscale in <u>Within the Cup</u>. "Thisbe Lorraine
warns the <u>Jap</u> servant not to tell."

In late January of 1918, Paralta announced the signing of Louise Glaum. "It is our intention," commented Robert Brunton in The Moving Picture World of February 9, 1918, "to give Miss Glaum roles which will bring into evidence her rare talents for fine sympathetic and emotional acting, and at the same time retain in her work those qualities which have won for her the exalted position she now enjoys. The element of sympathy and the widened emotional scope should earn her an added popularity."

Louise Glaum's director at Paralta was Wallace Worsley, who was later to be responsible for Lon Chaney's The Hunchback of Notre Dame. Glaum's first film for Paralta was An Enemy Allen, released by Hodkinson on April 1, 1918.* According to The Moving Picture World (April 27, 1918), An Alien Enemy was "intended to teach the people of the United States what the agents of the Kaiser are doing for him in this country and France." Glaum and Worsley followed An Alien Enemy with Wedlock, A Law Unto Herself and Shackled, among others.

On April 13, 1918, The Moving Picture World announced that work on the new Paralta studios, covering some ten acres of an eighty-acre tract at the corner of Melrose Avenue and Van Ness, was almost completed. The new studios were located directly opposite Paralta's first Los Angeles studios. The Moving Picture World reported, "Immediately facing Melrose Avenue will be the central administration building, flanked on either side by the buildings of the scenario department and the cafe. Behind these structures is the mammoth brick property building, separated by a central archway leading back to the five steel and glass-inclosed stages, each of which measures 60 x 150 feet, and which has ample stage space to accommodate six to eight settings. These stages are to be higher than any glass stages now in use, this being done to arrange for better manipulation of the light-duffusing system and to make possible the suspension of certain scenic effects from the supporting girders in the top of the structures."

Everything seemed well with Paralta. While Robert T. Kane was serving in the armed forces, Benjamin B. Hamp-

---

* The lack of release dates for Paralta productions is not deliberate. With its films being offered on the equivalent of a state's rights basis, release dates were seldom if ever published.

ton's brother, Jesse, was acting as Paralta's West Coast
business manager.   J. Warren Kerrigan had returned to the
Company after a long illness.   By May of 1918, Paralta had
produced eighteen features, none of which had been unfavor-
ably received by either critics or public.

Then, on May 7, 1918, it was announced that John E.
DeWolf and Herman Katz had acquired the Company, and
bought out the interests of Carl Anderson, Robert T. Kane
and Nat L. Brown.   According to The Moving Picture World
(May 25, 1918), "A complete reorganization has taken place,
and the Paralta Pictures Corporation is now in the strong
hands of well-known business men, who will continue the
making of photoplay offerings of exceptional merit."   Robert
Brunton remained as head of production, and it was announced
that each star under contract would make eight features a
year, to be released by the W. W. Hodkinson Corporation.

Certainly, Paralta did continue producing films for a
number of months, at least through to the late summer of
1918, but slowly the studios ceased to be Paralta's and became the Robert Brunton Studios.   Obviously the money men
realized the capabilities of Brunton, and that he would be
ideal to finance in the operation of a rental studio.   Hodkinson
and Brunton prospered--the latter was one of the most successful of the independent studio owners--but, by the end of
1918, Paralta's name had completely disappeared from the
pages of the trade papers.

It is a curious coincidence that the Paralta studios
became the Robert Brunton studios, and were eventually taken
over by Paramount, which occupies them to the present.   The
similarity in the names of the two companies, and the fact
that Hodkinson, who founded Paramount, should have gone
on to distribute the Paralta product is intriguing.   It is
almost as if Paralta, unbeknownst, had been Paramount's
alter ego.

10. THE O'KALEMS

The idea of American companies shooting films on
location abroad is not a new conception. Its genesis is with
the Kalem Company's excursions, first to Ireland and then
to the rest of Europe and the Middle East. Following closely
on the heels of Kalem was the Vitagraph Company, which in
December of 1912 sent Maurice Costello and others on a six-
month trip around the world, shooting wherever locations
seemed appropriate. Nor was there only a one-way traffic
from America abroad; the Pathé Company and Gaston Méliès'
Eclair Company were quick to seize the opportunity of setting
up companies in the United States. One might almost go so
far as to say that film-making was more international in the
'teens than at any other period in history, including the present.

It all began in the small, isolated County Kerry village of Beaufort, some seven miles from the Irish town of
Killarney. Beaufort holds a special place in the history of
the cinema, for it was here that the Kalem Company came
when they first decided to produce films outside of the United
States.

According to Terry Ramsaye's somewhat romanticized
account in A Million and One Nights, Frank Marion, president
of the Kalem Company, called director Sidney Olcott into his
office at the Kodak Building on New York's West 23 Street
in the Spring of 1910. On Marion's desk was a map of the
world. He asked Olcott where he would like to go and make
films; without hesitation, Olcott pointed to the country of his
ancestors, Ireland. (Olcott's mother was born in Dublin,
and the director's first stage appearance had been as an
Irish policeman in Joe Santley's company. As Gene Gauntier,
Kalem's leading lady and scenario writer, once wrote of
Olcott: "He was Irish and possessed all the sparkle and
sentiment of that emotional race.")

In August 1910, Sidney Olcott, with Gene Gauntier,

Robert Vignola, and cameraman George Hollister, landed at
the Irish port of Queenstown, now called Cobh. They stayed
for a short while at the Victoria Hotel, Cork, and then moved
to the Glebe Hotel, Killarney. Olcott did not find the town
of Killarney appealing. He thought the citizens too concerned
with the amount of money to be made from the tourists--a
fault which they have to this day--and so determined to find
a more pleasant spot at which to stay and film. One day,
while out touring the country in a jaunting car, he stumbled
upon the village of Beaufort, and decided it was ideal for his
requirements.

Olcott's efforts to explain to the villagers what he
wanted caused some amusement. The people of Beaufort
had never seen a motion picture. Olcott asked them if they
had been present at a magic lantern show. Yes, they knew
about magic lantern entertainments. "Well," said Olcott,
"Films are like magic lantern slides, but they move." The
inhabitants were just as bewildered as when Olcott had first
approached them, but were willing to help the director on
his first Irish production, The Lad from Old Ireland.

The company also shot film of a number of Irish beauty
spots, including Blarney Castle, Glengariffe and, of course,
the Lakes of Killarney, which was edited together into a one-
reeler titled The Irish Honeymoon. Leaving Beaufort, the
company went on to Germany, where they filmed portions of
The Little Spreewald Maiden.

Like The Little Spreewald Maiden, part of The Lad
from Old Ireland was shot in New York, and when Kalem
released the film on November 23, 1910 it was advertised
as "the first drama ever made on two continents." The
Moving Picture World (December 3, 1910) commented, "It
is the story of an Irish boy who comes to America to seek
his fortune, finds it and returns to Ireland in time to save
his sweetheart from eviction. Its chief interest lies in the
scenery. Probably most audiences will enjoy it, and of
course the Irish lad will make the Irish portion of any audience hilarious."

The Irish Honeymoon was not released until March
of 1911. According to The Moving Picture World (March 25,
1911), it consisted of "a series of excellent pictures, showing
what Ireland is like in its most picturesque portions. It
closes with a visit to the estate of Richard Croker, giving
a view of that gentleman himself in the act of receiving the
honeymooners. This photography has been admirably done,

the viewpoints having been selected by an artist of ability."

Just as The Lad from Old Ireland and The Irish Honeymoon were produced with a view to appealing to Irish immigrants, so was The Little Spreewald Maiden intended for America's German population. The Moving Picture World (December 31, 1910) was quick to note, "Wherever there are Germans, this film should be popular."

Surprisingly, however, Kalem did not decide to repeat the German experiment. Instead, on July 3, 1911, Sidney Olcott and a group of Kalem players and technicians again set sail from New York for Ireland on the R. M. S. Baltic. The company included Arthur Donaldson, Fred Santley, Agnes Mapes (who also acted as wardrobe mistress), Jack Clark, Robert Vignola (who also acted as assistant director), Alice Hollister, J. P. McGowan, and Gene Gauntier. George Hollister was again the cameraman, and Allen Farnham was responsible for the sets.

The O'Kalems, as they were nicknamed on their second visit to Ireland, arrived on the "ould sod" on June 10, and by July 1, The Moving Picture World reported they were quartered in Beaufort. The Moving Picture World noted that "on the trip over the O'Kalems could not forget work and to keep up their reputation produced a very laughable comedy. In this picture they were aided and abetted by several of the officers of the steamer and a number of the passengers."

At Beaufort, the O'Kalems stayed with Patrick O'Sullivan and his daughter, Annie.* The company built a platform in the field behind the O'Sullivan's home, and here many of the interior scenes were filmed. So primitive were conditions at Beaufort that the company also built an outside bathroom for their use, in the same field.

The O'Kalems were happy with the O'Sullivans, and vice versa. In a letter to her brother in New York, Agnes Mapes wrote, "It was very cold last night, and we had our peat fire in the old fireplace in our little parlor with its crooked leg piano, and Jack Clark played his violin and we all sang until bedtime." In one of her letters home, Gene Gauntier commented, "Oh dear Lord, how beautiful it is!

---

* Some of the anecdotes and incidents included in this essay were described to me by Annie O'Sullivan during a visit to Beaufort in the Spring of 1967.

And over it all, the stillness, the brooding melancholy, the sad heart-touching loveliness that belongs only to Ireland. Sometimes, when I throw myself face down in the thick green grass of the 'Fairy Ring' which crowns our pasture, I am sure I can hear her heart beat through the silence that enfolds me."

The first production which the O'Kalems made in Beaufort that year was Rory O'More, the story of an eighteenth-century Irish revolutionary hero. Jack Clark played the title role, with Gene Gauntier as his sweetheart, Kathleen, Arthur Donaldson as the militant priest, and Robert Vignola as The Informer. At the film's release on September 4, 1911, The Moving Picture World (August 19, 1911) published a two-page review in which it commented, "Photographically it approaches perfection to a degree that is unusual, and several pleasing and novel effects point to the photographer's skill and ingenuity."

The Sunday after the film was completed, the O'Sullivans, with Sidney Olcott, Robert Vignola, Jack Clark and his mother, and Alice Hollister attended mass at the local Catholic church. Vignola recalled--in a 1953 Radio Eireann interview--that the priest finished reading from the gospels, and "with a grim look on his face and a menacing tone in his voice" attacked the film-makers in his midst. He called them "tramp photographers," whose films were intended "to degrade the Irish." He noted they filmed in the churchyard and were "desecrating the bones of our ancestors," and that "many of our fine lads were marching around in the uniforms of old English soldiers, selling their souls to the devils for a few paltry shillings."

The villagers were shocked, as were the O'Kalems, and filming could not continue until Olcott and the American consul in Queenstown had been to see the local Bishop, who ordered the parish priest to apologize for his remarks. It later transpired that the priest had made his remarks after being approached by local traders whose businesses were being ruined by tourists going off to watch the filming instead of patronizing their shops.

The O'Kalems had a busy time in Beaufort, producing many films, including The O'Neill, released on January 12, 1912; His Mother, released on January 26, 1912; You Remember Ellen, released on March 4, 1912; The O'Kalems Visit to Killarney, released on January 5, 1912; Far from Erin's Eye, released on February 14, 1912; and The Franciscan

<u>Friars of Killarney</u>, released on November 29, 1911.

Most importantly, the O'Kalems produced two major
films based on the plays of Dion Boucicault, <u>The Colleen
Bawn</u> and <u>Arrah-na-Pogue</u>. Starring Gene Gauntier as Eily
O'Connor, the Colleen, and Jack Clark as Myles na Cop-
paleen, <u>The Colleen Bawn</u> was released, in three reels, on
October 16, 1911. The director, Sidney Olcott, portrayed
the simple-minded cripple, Danny Mann. Olcott's acting
received much praise; <u>The Moving Picture World</u> (September
30, 1911) wrote, "In giving expression to this quaint character, Mr. Olcott has done more than to portray mere exter-
nals--he has given us a glimpse of the very soul of the unfortunate Danny, which portrayal reaches its climax in the
confession scene in the third part--a bit of playing that
fairly speaks out from the screen."

<u>The Moving Picture World</u> devoted two pages to a re-
view of <u>The Colleen Bawn</u>, describing it as "the chef d'oeuvre
of American motion picture production." Continued <u>The
World</u>, "Out of this lavish outpouring of capital and the devotion to duty of the players comes, among others, the picture story of <u>The Colleen Bawn</u> as a most fitting climax to
a high endeavor, not alone typical of the company immediately
concerned, but of American picture making as an enterprise,
alert, resourceful and progressive."

Kalem's <u>The Colleen Bawn</u> was not the first film version of the Boucicault play--it had been produced earlier in
1911 by the Yankee Film Company--but it was certainly the
most popular. It was reissued in February of 1914, and at
that time the company devised a novel publicity stunt to pro-
mote the production. Several tons of Irish soil, from the
base of the Colleen Bawn rock on Lake Killarney, were ship-
ped--on the <u>S. S. Megantic</u>--to New York. The soil was por-
tioned out into trays, four feet square and one inch deep,
and these trays were distributed with the film. Thus, patrons
attending screenings of <u>The Colleen Bawn</u> were also presented
with the unique opportunity to literally stand on Irish soil.

<u>Arrah-na-Pogue</u>, released on November 21, 1911, in
three reels, again featured Gene Gauntier, Jack Clark and
Sidney Olcott. <u>The Moving Picture World</u> (November 18,
1911) commented, "There is not a dull moment in the entire
three reels of this subject and there are many situations
that are intensely gripping. For sustained action it is the
best three-reel subject we have seen up-to-date." Composer,
Walter Cleveland Simon was engaged by the Kalem Company

to write a special four-piece orchestral score for the film.

On Friday, October 6, 1911, the O'Kalems returned to New York. Missing from their company was Arthur Donaldson, who had left Ireland for Sweden, where he was to undertake a year's theatrical engagement. Immediately upon their return, the O'Kalems were given a dinner party, at which Eugene V. Brewster, managing editor of The Motion Picture Story Magazine, gave an address of welcome. For a while, it looked as if the O'Kalems were to lose their director, for Sidney Olcott had expressed a desire to leave the company. Gene Gauntier was about to take over directorial duties when Frank Marion announced that a new contract with Olcott had been worked out.

From New York, the O'Kalems moved to Jacksonville, Florida, to spend the winter. Their stay in Florida was brief, for on December 2, they departed the United States again, this time for Egypt and Palestine. It was on this trip, which lasted through the early summer of 1912, that Sidney Olcott and Gene Gauntier produced From the Manger to the Cross. It was a production widely praised in its day, but strangely unpopular with the friends of the O'Kalems in Beaufort. The portrayal of the Virgin Mary by a divorced woman--Gene Gauntier--was considered sacrilegious. (At the time of her Irish productions, Gene Gauntier was married to Jack Clark.)

While the O'Kalems were in Egypt, Frank Marion acquired the rights to further "Irish" plays. Dion Boucicault's The Shaughraun was the first new work to come under Kalem's control, and it was followed by two plays of Joseph Murphy, The Kerry Gow and Shaun Rhue. Despite their age--both Murphy plays had been touring the United States for thirty years--the Kalem Company had no doubts as to their value. The Moving Picture World (May 25, 1912) reported that "Mr. Murphy has co-operated with Kalem, furnishing many details of 'business' which made his plays so successful."

In July of 1912, the O'Kalems returned to Ireland for what was to be their last visit as members of the Kalem Company. In an article in The Moving Picture World of August 10, 1912, J. P. McGowan wrote, "Ireland is almost like a second home to us, and as we drove out to the Gap [of Dunloe] on the same old cars, behind the same old horses, we found that the folks had heard of our return and familiar faces beamed forth a hearty welcome as we came into view. At Beaufort itself there was a regular reunion. Everybody

was present, the postman on his way home dropped in for a
moment, the blacksmith from the village came in to pass
'th' time o'day' and even Brandy, a real Irish terrier, remembered us, and almost wagged his stump of a tail during
the first few hours and, satisfied we were back, he came
into his own again and appropriated the door mat leading into
the dining-room, from which he had been banished for months
past."

Among the Kalem productions filmed in Ireland during
1912 were The Mayor from Ireland, released on November 30,
1912; Conway, the Kerry Dancer, released on December 9,
1912; Ireland the Oppressed, released on December 14, 1912;
and Lady Peggy's Escape, released on February 8, 1913.

Starring Jack Clark as Dan O'Hara and Alice Hollister
as Nora Drew, The Kerry Gow was released, in three reels,
on November 18, 1912. W. Stephen Bush in The Moving
Picture World (November 9, 1912) wrote: "There is nothing
new or startling about the plot of the play. It is of that
ancient pattern wherein the villain seeks to wrest the beautiful daughter from the bosom of the hero just because he
holds the mortgage on the father's cottage. The story ends
with the villain on his way to jail and the lovers getting ready
for the marriage feast. The charm and power of this version
of the old play come from the romantic little by-plays so
dear to the Irish heart, the displays of Irish humor veering
from the subtle to the rollicking and back again and always
close to the fountain of tears, from the singular idyllic charm
of the Irish landscape, from the excellent acting and the un-
mistakable air of realism with which this company has invested all its Irish plays. The attention to details, without
which a play like this would lose much on its way from the
stage to the celluloid, does infinite credit to the director.
When the action of the play calls for the interior of a country
lawyer's office, nothing will do but a real interior of a country lawyer's office to which the camera pays a careful visit.
A real 'Dan' works in a real blacksmith shop and even the
'Dinny Doyle,' who peers over the fence and hears the villains
plotting and rejoicing, is the kind that you would expect to
meet on an Irish country road on a workday's afternoon."

The Shaughraun, released in three reels on December
25, 1912, was particularly well received. Sidney Olcott, as
Conn, the Shaughraun, was highly praised, and he received
excellent support from Jack Clark, Robert Melville, J. P.
McGowan, and Gene Gauntier. W. Stephen Bush's review in
The Moving Picture World (December 14, 1912) is well worth

quoting at length:

> "In the galaxy of features known as the O'Kalem plays, this production shines out with especial lustre. It embodies all the profits of previous experience. When this company began filming Irish plays on Irish soil it entered a new field of cinematographic endeavor. It demonstrated beyond all cavil that the motion picture is vastly more than a mere vehicle of cheap dramatic composition. Because of its efforts we can challenge the novelist, the historian and the dramatist to a combat of portrayal and description with no fear of the result for the prestige and superiority of the motion picture.

> "The Shaughraun shows an unwearied ambition on the part of the Kalems. They have in this production striven even more earnestly and have aimed even more skillfully and conscientiously than in any of their other Irish subjects, splendid as they all are. In The Shaughraun, it seems to me, they have well-nigh touched perfection in the use they made of outdoor scenery. Nothing in art or literature can approach the ability of the gifted and painstaking producer in creating atmosphere. After we have seen the weird and rugged beauty of the stern and cliff-bound Irish coast, much of the temperament and much in the history of the Celtic race becomes as clear as crystal. We enjoy the sensation. We thrill with delight at this new way of learning things by the roots. If these three magnificent reels had not a single point of merit but the choice they made of characteristic stretches of this wild and romantic coast, they would be well worth seeing. Imposing, however, as all these scenes are, they form but a part of the true story and the true atmosphere, and we feel constantly that they have been selected for that purpose only. The selection does high credit to the director. I have seen splendid outdoor scenery in motion picture plays, but my enjoyment was greatly lessened by the fact that the producer evidently counted on the scenery to 'pull through' a time-worn plot or a lot of amateurish actors and actresses. The Shaughraun gives us its scenic splendors as merely one item in its program of uniform excellence."

The O'Kalems, after a brief visit to England and Scotland, returned to New York from Liverpool, England, on October 3, 1912. But all was not well between the O'Kalems and the Kalem management. The company seemed displeased with From the Manger to the Cross, and decided to release it minus player or technical cre-

dits.* Olcott, Gauntier, Jack Clark, and Allen Farnham resigned from the company. "Our notices," wrote Gene Gauntier,
"were accepted with unflattering alacrity and we were thanked,
but behind the expressed good wishes we had the feeling that
the Kalem Company was relieved at our desertion."

At this point, it is perhaps worth noting that Lewis
Jacobs, in The Rise of the American Film, claims that several of the Irish productions of the Kalem Company displeased
the British authorities. Despite such blatantly pro-Irish in-
dependence, anti-British occupation films as Rory O'More
and The O'Neill, Kalem's activities seem to have aroused
little concern. The films were released in England and
Ireland without incident. On November 5, 1911, Rory O'More
was the inaugural film in a series of Sunday performances
at Dublin's Volta Electric Theatre, a theatre which is of
particular interest as its manager was one James Joyce.

When The O'Neill was released in England on February 25, 1912, the British trade periodical The Bioscope
described its plot, concerning an Irish patriot who takes to
highway robbery to raise money for the cause of Irish free-
dom, as "picturesque, romantic and altogether delightful."
After the 1916 Easter Rebellion in Dublin, Kalem reissued
The O'Neill under the title of The Irish Rebel.

Kalem's Irish productions were undoubtedly popular
with all ethnic groups, not just Irish immigrants. Even after
the disbandment of the O'Kalems, Kalem produced at least
one "Irish" film, The Octoroon, released on December 1,
1913. Produced in Florida, and probably directed by Kenean
Buel, it featured Guy Coombs and Marguerite Courtot. The
Octoroon was, of course, based on the popular melodrama
of the same name by Dion Boucicault.

To all extents and purposes, the story of the O'Kalems
ends here. The question arises as to how good the O'Kalem
productions were in relation to other films of the period.
Trade paper reports indicate that they were superior to most
other film product. The few Kalem Irish productions which
have survived, including Rory O'More and The Colleen Bawn,
indicate Olcott's directorial skills in the natural use of loca-

---

* Cecil B. DeMille's 1927 production of King of Kings was
also released without player or technical credits on the film,
and the reason was undoubtedly the religious nature of the
production.

tions; the sunlight dappled on the brick wall of an old Irish cottage, the opening shot from The Colleen Bawn of the main square of Beaufort. Sidney Olcott's Irish productions certainly earned him his title of "The Belasco of the Open Air."

"So our family of pathfinders disbanded, as pioneers will do when the long trail is ended," wrote Gene Gauntier. "And each are departed into new environments, to build for himself. As settlers in a new land, some were submerged while others went blithely on to the top crest of popularity. Life never stood still, nor would we wish it to. Suffice for us the memories of that epoch in our lives, with its joys and its sorrows, its thrills and adventures, its affections and achievements. We would not live through them again, nor yet would we desire to part with the memories of those days when we were blazing the trail."

The story does not quite end there, for on December 21, 1912, The Moving Picture World announced the formation of The Gene Gauntier Feature Players Company, which was to release its productions through Warner's Features. The Company, consisting of Gene Gauntier, Sidney Olcott, Jack Clark, and Allen Farnham, immediately left for Jacksonville, Florida, and was able to join Kalem's Southern Company for Christmas dinner there. It was no surprise when the Gene Gauntier Feature Players Company, "the Gee Gees," became "the O'Gees," and embarked on the S.S. Adriatic for Ireland on August 14, 1913. During their stay in Beaufort--shorter than in the O'Kalem days--the company produced For Ireland's Sake, released on January 12, 1914, and Come Back to Erin, released in March of 1914.

Sidney Olcott resigned from the Gene Gauntier Feature Players Company in January of 1914, but it remained in existence for a further year, until the spring of 1915, when Gene Gauntier and Jack Clark became members of the Universal Company. Olcott formed Sid Films, and with his new leading lady and future wife, Valentine Grant, returned to Beaufort for the last time in the summer of 1914. The Company included Pat O'Malley, Laurene Santley, Arthur Donaldson, Jack Melville and Robert Rivers, along with cameraman Hal Young. Olcott produced a number of films in Ireland, including The Irish in America and Bold Emmett, Ireland's Martyr, which were not released until 1915 by the Lubin Company. Had not the First World War engulfed Europe, Sidney Olcott and his players might have returned again to Beaufort. The residents of the village recall that Olcott had spoken of creating a permanent film studio there, and that he told them

the Irish were natural actors and actresses. The mild County
Kerry climate--it never snows--would have been ideal for
year-round filming.

No members of the O'Kalems are alive today. When
Valentine Grant died on March 12, 1949, Sidney Olcott went
to live with his old Kalem companion, Robert Vignola. A
few weeks before Christmas of that year, Olcott wrote out
his Christmas cards and parceled up his wife's jewelry, to
be sent to individuals to whom he felt Val would want them
to go. On December 16, Olcott told Vignola that he felt ill,
and went to his room to rest. Vignola wrote, "At 4.45pm
I looked at my watch and decided to wake him. His face
was blue and his eyes were staring into space. I called to
him. Somehow I felt he had heard me and made an effort
to move. He was dead when the doctor arrived."

A few days before Christmas, Annie O'Sullivan received
two letters in the mail. The first was from Vignola, telling
her of Olcott's death. The other was from Olcott, and contained a gold bracelet which had belonged to his wife. He
had never forgotten Beaufort.

11. EARLY FILM MAGAZINES: AN OVERVIEW

For anyone studying the early years of American cinema, the most important research books are the film periodicals of the era, and researchers are lucky that so many were published, and that so many have survived. There were fan magazines and film company house journals galore but, most importantly, there were also many trade publications.

Without question, among the trade periodicals, the most valuable from a research point of view today is The Moving Picture World. It featured the most detailed news items, the best reviews and feature articles, particularly by Louis Reeves Harrison, W. Stephen Bush and George Blaisdell, and a vast advertisement section, which can offer the researcher untold treasures. The Moving Picture World began publication on March 9, 1907, and appeared weekly until January 7, 1928, when it became Exhibitors Herald and Moving Picture World. Interestingly, the cover of the first issue of the new magazine featured an advertisement for Metro-Goldwyn-Mayer, headed "Mergers Make Greatness!" There was one break in publication during The Moving Picture World's life; no issues appeared between October 4 and November 8, 1919.

(The Moving Picture World, happily, is available to anyone on microfilm from the Library of Congress, and it is worth noting that the American Film Institute has published an index, compiled by Rita Horwitz, to volume one of the magazine. One of the most important projects still to be undertaken in the field of film history research is a complete index to The Moving Picture World.)

The Moving Picture World's chief competitor was Motion Picture News. All too many writers on film history confuse the two, and make reference to The Motion Picture World. Motion Picture News began publication in 1908 as Moving Picture News. It became Motion Picture News with the issue of October 11, 1913, and continued publication under that name until January 3, 1931 when it combined with Exhibitors Herald and Moving Picture World to become Motion Picture Herald. Peter Milne was possibly the best known writer with Motion Picture News.

Two lesser trade periodicals were Motography and Exhibitor's Trade Review. The latter, which began publication on December 9, 1916, was a high-class trade periodical which deserves more attention, but of which, unfortunately, it is hard to locate substantial runs. Exhibitor's Trade Review featured detailed credits and synopses for each film it reviewed, and was also very much an admirer of D. W. Griffith. One can find more coverage on the director in this publication than in any other. Wid's (later to become Film) Daily made its appearance in the mid 'teens, and offered an honest, unbiased approach to film reviewing, but there was always something unbearably dull about Wid's and it is hard to be too enthusiastic.

For the years before 1910, there were a number of periodicals. Devoted exclusively to film were The Nickelodeon and Views and Film Index, which later became The Film Index. The New York Morning Telegraph, The New York Clipper, and Billboard all provided a certain amount of coverage of film matters, as did Variety. However, the last did not begin to devote the last few pages of each issue to motion pictures until 1913. It is curious to note that whereas vaudeville and the legitimate stage warranted the most number of pages and the front section of Variety during the 'teens and before, today film takes up almost the first half of the paper, while the legitimate stage might make two pages somewhere towards the rear, and vaudeville is but a memory. Biased as it obviously must have been, there is some truth in the comment by The Film Index (October 1, 1910): "While Variety is a good vaudeville paper--the best ever--it has always managed to get the wrong dope on the picture business. We do not recall that it has ever printed the correct version of any story. Bad showing for a paper that is so good in other things. "

Variety's biggest competitor was The New York Dramatic Mirror, which took an interest in film long before Variety did. Frank E. Woods must receive full credit for the success of The New York Dramatic Mirror; he created the Moving Picture Department, and offered the first serious film reviews by a trade paper. However, by the late 'teens, long after Woods had left, the review section of The New York Dramatic Mirror had become almost a joke, with few credits and little serious comment.

As far as honesty in reviewing goes, Variety really deserves credit for admitting that films were produced to make money, and should be criticized with that in mind. Typical of Variety's comments is the following from its November 28, 1913 review of Victim of Sin: "Heading for Broadway via Italy and the 57th Street branch of Manhattan's Y.M.-C.A., this new chamber of horrors should make a cargo of money for its promoters, offering as it does in movies all the essentials of the Brieux drama, Damaged Goods, and carrying to the innocent and the informed dramatic and tragic consequences of promiscuous sex relations." Variety could also demolish a reputation in a single paragraph, as the following from its August 1, 1919 edition illustrates: "Mary MacLane, heroine of the frenzied film, Men Who Have Made Love to Me, and of the sensational book, I, Mary MacLane, was arrested at her home this week on a charge of larceny by bailee. It seems that Alla Ripley, the modiste, had furnished certain gowns for Mary when she was putting the picture on, which were neither returned nor paid for, the complainant alleged. Having only 85 cents to her name, I, Mary, was pinched."

In Britain, as in the States, two trade periodicals led the field: The Bioscope and The Kinematograph Weekly. The Kine, as it was affectionately called, was founded on June 15, 1889, as The Optical Magic Lantern Journal and Photographic Enlarger, under the editorship of J. Hay Taylor. In November 1904 the name was changed to The Optical Lantern and Cinematograph Journal, and in May 1907, under the editorship of Theodore Brown, it became The Kinematograph and Lantern Weekly. The heyday of The Kine was in the Twenties, under the editorship of Frank Tilley.* The Kinematograph Weekly disappeared on September 25, 1971, when it was combined with Today's Cinema, which was founded in 1912 as The Cinema News and Property Gazette, and which has now also gone under. The Kinematograph Weekly also published, during the 'teens and Twenties, The Kinematograph Monthly Film Record, a useful checklist of current releases, similar to the Motion Picture News' Booking Guides.

The Bioscope was first published on September 18, 1908 and ceased on May 4, 1932, when it was amalgamated

---

* See this author's interview with Tilley, under the title of "Farewell Kine," in The Silent Picture (Winter-Spring, 1972).

with The Kinematograph Weekly. Of the two, The Bioscope is probably the most reliable, but researchers should bear in mind that much of its reporting on the American scene was lifted from American trade papers.

Competition between The Bioscope and The Kinematograph Weekly was not always friendly. The Kine was published by E. T. Heron--in its last years it was owned by I. P. C. Heron was the subject of an extraordinary editorial in The Bioscope of May 27, 1909. Under a heading, "Edward Thomas Heron and His Sneaking Way," The Bioscope accused Heron of sending "secret enquiries" to its printers as to the ownership of the magazine. The editorial ended by suggesting, "Our own advice to Edward Thomas Heron is that he should give more attention to his little stationer's shop, where he so admirably fills his role of public usefulness in the dispensing of penny bottles of ink and ha'porths of envelopes. If he minds his own business and ceases to worry about us, he, too, may one day become a successful publisher."

Britain also boasted its fair share of fan magazines in the 'teens. The most popular were Pictures and the Picturegoer and Picture Show, neither of which was too wonderful, and certainly both are totally unreliable for research purposes. There was also Illustrated Films Monthly, published in the early 'teens, which appears to have been modeled after the American Motion Picture Story Magazine. Several British film distributors published their own magazines; Stoll had Stoll's Editorial News and Walturdaw had the Walturdaw Weekly Budget. Most importantly, the Motion Picture Sales Corporation, which distributed Kalem, Lubin and American Biograph products in Britain, published Top Line Indicator, which listed player credits and succinct synopses for films during 1912 and 1913.

Most, if not all, American producers published periodicals detailing information on their new releases, together with articles on their contract stars. Some of the earliest were The Edison Kinetogram, Vitagraph Life Portrayals, Eclair News, Essanay News and Essanay Guide, Kalem Kalendar, Lubin Bulletin, the New York Motion Picture Company's Film Fancies, the IMP Company's Implet, and The Biograph, which did not come into existence until after D. W. Griffith had left the Company. The Universal Weekly, which became The Moving Picture Weekly for a while in the mid-'teens, is a mine of information. In 1917, the William Fox Company began publication of Exhibitors Bulletin; Selznick published Motion Picture Times; Triangle published The

Triangle and Triangle News; Mutual published Reel Life; and Pathé published Pathé Messenger, which superseded Pathé-plays. Even the Christie Comedy Company had its own house organ, Film Follies, and the Selig Company produced a journal strictly for use in the journalistic field and called it Paste-Pot and Shears.

One of the most elegant of the early house journals was Paramount Progress, first published December 3, 1914, under the editorship of J. S. Johnson. Motion Picture News (December 12, 1914) noted, "Paramount Progress is most attractively printed on a superior quality of paper and bears every mark of refinement." In July 1915 it became Paramount Magazine, and when Artcraft appeared on the scene, it became Paramount Artcraft Progressive Advance.

By the late 'teens, educational film magazines such as Educational Film Magazine and Reel and Slide had appeared. Aimed at the classroom and church audience, they offer nothing of value to researchers. The National Board of Review of Motion Pictures produced a magazine with the delightful title of A Garden of American Motion Pictures, concerned with wholesome films for the family. One fascinating publication, of which I have seen only two extant issues, was Static Flashes, edited by Captain Jack Poland and produced during 1915 by, I presume, an early cameraman's association called The Static Club of America. "Devoted to the men who make the movies," it featured nothing but news items and articles such as "How I Became a Motion Picture Director" by Lois Weber and "Reliance-Majestic-Griffith-Studios" by Bennie Zeidman. Another cinematography-oriented publication--this time from the late 'teens--was Camera, which is particularly valuable for information on films in production, plus camera and assistant director credits.

Fan magazines comprise the bulk of the early periodicals. * The leader in the field was Photoplay (founded in 1912), closely followed by Motion Picture Magazine (founded in February 1911 by J. Stuart Blackton and Eugene V. Brewster as Motion Picture Story Magazine) and its sister publication, Motion Picture Classic. In Chicago, during 1915 and 1916, Feature Movie Magazine was published. Picture-Play magazine contains some interesting articles, including

---

* For more information on fan magazines, see this author's The Idols of Silence (A. S. Barnes, 1976) and my introduction to Ten Years in Paradise (The Pleasant Press, 1974).

a lengthy biography of Thomas Ince, published between January and June 1917. Picture-Play began publication on April 10, 1915 as a weekly, soon became a bi-monthly, and finally settled down to a long run as a monthly. There were Movie Pictorial, Movies Weekly, and Photo-Play World, a beautifully-produced but short-lived periodical from the mid-teens.

Photo-Play World was followed by Photo-Play Journal, "a magazine with a heart, a soul and character." It was edited by Delbert E. Davenport, who also doubled as the magazine's film critic, Bert D. Essex. Gorgeously produced, Photo-Play Journal is interesting because it featured the first writings on cinema by Edward Wagenknecht, and included an advice column, titled "For You and Me," handled by Madame Olga Petrova.

Most writing in fan magazines is suspect; all too often in the 'teens one finds that articles on individuals or studios were written by their own publicists. Yet Photoplay demonstrated some integrity with its critics, Julian Johnson and later Burns Mantle. (Edward Wagenknecht points out that it is doubtful that Burns Mantle ever really understood the difference between a play and a film.) Hazel Simpson Naylor and Frederick James Smith of Motion Picture Magazine and Motion Picture Classic were good, but they are not in the same league as Johnson and Mantle.

There is an interesting insight into Smith and Naylor in a letter from Harry Carr, a fine writer associated with the Los Angeles Times for many years, to D. W. Griffith, and dated December of 1918: "I found him [Frederick James Smith] to be a shy, diffident boy in the early twenties .... He said that The Great Love had given him the opinion that D. W. G. was slipping, etc. --a conclusion helped out perhaps by the fact that Maurice Tourneur has employed him to do some press stuff .... Miss Naylor is a sweet, attractive little girl of about 22. She is a Smith College graduate; comes from a very fine Buffalo family and is a lot smarter than Smith."

A splendid example of why the integrity of early fan magazines is in doubt is the case of Moving Picture Stories, which began publication on January 3, 1913. It basically consisted of adaptations of half-a-dozen or so short fictional films, and a couple of articles on a specific star or director. However, a careful study of Moving Picture Stories reveals that virtually all the films, stars and directors covered came from Universal, and many of the articles also appeared in

The Universal Weekly, sometimes under different bylines. It is not hard to guess that Moving Picture Stories was published, albeit surreptitiously, by Universal.

In summation, any serious research into early American cinema must be conducted through the pages of The Moving Picture World, but a careful reading of Variety and The New York Dramatic Mirror on the side would not come amiss. If I were to be stranded on the proverbial desert island and could take only two further periodicals with me, one fan and one house organ, my choice would be Photoplay and The Universal Weekly.

12. THE FIRST MOTION PICTURE BIBLIOGRAPHY

The first motion picture bibliography appeared not in one of the major film trade papers--Variety, The Moving Picture World or The New York Dramatic Mirror--but in the lesser known Motography, in its issue of August 5, 1916. Compiled by S. Gershanek, a cataloger with the Reference Division of the New York State Public Library, this bibliography listed some 120 books and pamphlets on the motion picture.

Not surprisingly, the largest percentage of the publications listed dealt with writing for the photoplay, indicative of that period when writing for the movies seemed more accessible to fans than acting in movies. Of all the books listed on this subject, it is doubtful that any have lasting value, although it is interesting to note a book on How to Write for the Movies by Louella Parsons from 1915. In fact, reading through the bibliography, one is struck by how few books listed are now considered of any worth. Certainly Robert Grau's The Theater of Science is one of the most important books on early cinema, as is Vachel Lindsay's The Art of the Moving Picture, which Gershanek obviously had difficulty categorizing, and eventually placed under "miscellaneous," but how many of the other volumes have stood the test of time? One major omission from the bibliography is Frances Agnew's Motion Picture Acting (1913), important for its interviews with early players such as John Bunny and Alice Joyce.

A considerable number of foreign-language publications are listed; twenty-seven in German and six in French. One major foreign language work which stands out is film pioneer Georges Demeny's Les Origines du Cinématographie.

It is interesting to compare this 1916 bibliography with one published in the July 1920 issue of the Monthly Bulletin of the St. Louis Public Library. The latter contains a con-

105

siderable number of periodical references which Gershanek ignores completely, but few major books have appeared in the intervening years. There are A. C. Lescarboura's Behind the Motion Picture Screen (1919) and Geoffrey Malin's How I Filmed the War, but that is about it.

The St. Louis Public Library bibliography does include one or two pre-1916 books which are not in the Motography bibliography, including what must have been a fascinating study by J. N. Risley on The Effect of Moving Pictures on the Eyes (1915). Apparently, eye-strain from watching motion pictures was quite a concern at that time; the Literary Digest for May 30, 1914 contained an article on "Eye-strain from the Movie Habit," and in its issue of July 31, 1915 returned to the subject with "Movies and the Eyes." (Of course, Motography being a film industry publication, it is rather obvious why eye-strain should have been ignored by its bibliographer.)

It is indicative of the influence of motion pictures on the community by 1920 that not only did the St. Louis Public Library publish such a bibliography, but also that it devoted six pages of its Bulletin to the effort. In 1918, both Library Journal and Publisher's Weekly began listing novels that had been filmed, a sure sign that the world of literature had accepted the world of film-making, both as an education aid (by Library Journal) and as a source of income (Publisher's Weekly).

"A Motion Picture Bibliography," compiled by S. Gershanek, is reprinted below, exactly as it appeared in Motography, August 5, 1916 (Volume XII, Number 6), pages 339-342. No attempt has been made to correct probable errors.

A Motion Picture Bibliography

Compiled by S. Gershanek, A. M.

Cataloguer, Reference Division New York State Public Library, Photoplaywright, Ex-Photoplay Editor and Research Director.

In the following list Motography presents the most complete and up-to-date catalogue of books and pamphlets on motion pictures and its related fields which has ever been published. This list has been prepared to meet the needs of the motion picture manufacturer, his producing directors, and editors; the exhibitors; the photoplaywright, staff and free lance; or others employed or interested in moving pictures.

The compiler will be pleased to receive catalogues of supply companies to add to a later list, and will be pleased to hear from any and all writers on any subject of interest to the field for insertion in this catalogue. At various intervals additional titles and corrections will appear in the issues of Motography.

Motion Pictures-Educational Aspects

Bureau of Commercial Economics
    Bureau of Commercial Economics, Department of Public Instruction, Washington-Philadelphia, Ferris & Leach. Copyrighted 1915; 48 pages.

Ducom, Jacques
    Le cinématographie scientifique et industriel. Traite pratique de cinematographie. Paris, L. Geisler. Copyrighted 1911; 335 pages; illustrated.

Gaupp, Robert Eugen, and Lange, Konrad
    Der Kinematograph als Volksunterhaltungsmittel. Contents: Gaupp, R. E. Kinematograph von medizinischen und psychologischen Standpunkt. Lange, K. Der Kinematograph vom ethischen und asthetischen Standpunkt. Vertrage (Munchen, 1912); 50 pages.

Haefker, Hermann (1873)
    Kino und Erkunde-M. Gladbach. Copyrighted 1914; 78 pages. (Lichtbuhnen-Bibliothek. Nr. 7.)

Hannon, William Morgan
    The Photodrama; Its Place Among the Fine Arts. New Orleans, Ruskin Press. Copyrighted 1915; 68 pages.

Jump, Herbert A.
    The Religious Possibilities of the Motion Picture. (New Britain, Conn.) Printed for private distribution; 1910; 32 pages.

Kleine, George
    Catalogue of Educational Motion Picture Films-Licensed

by the Motion Picture Patents Company. Chicago, Press of Bentley, Murray & Co. Copyrighted 1910; 337 pages.

Knospe, Paul
Der Kinematograph im Dienste der Schule. Unter besonderer Berucksichtigung des erkundlichen Unterrichts. Halle a. d. S., 1913; 34 pages.

Lemke, Hermann
Die Kinematographs der Gegenwart, Vergangenheit und Kuzunft. Eine kulturgeschichte und industrielle Studie. Leipzig, E. Denne; copyrighted 1913; 56 pages.

Louisiana State University
Auto-stereopticon and moving picture machine for extension service in rural schools. Baton Rouge, 1915. (University Bulletin, new series, No. 7.)

Muensterberg, Hugo
The Photoplay; A Psychological Study. Contents: Introduction-The outer development of the moving pictures. The inner development of the moving pictures. Part 1: The psychology of the photoplay. Depth and movement. Attention. Memory and imagination. Emotions. Part II: The esthetics of the photoplay. The purpose of art. The means of the photoplay. The demands of the photoplay. The function of the photoplay. (D. Appleton & Co., New York. Copyrighted 1916; 232 pages.)

Pathe Freres
Descriptions of Moving Picture Films. New York. Copyrighted 1909; 7 pamphlets. Contents: Assassination of the Duke of Guise. The Hunter's Grief. Incriminating Evidence. The Kiss of Judas. The Return of Ulysses. La Tosca.

Philip, Alexander J.
Cinematograph Films; Their National Value and Preservation. London, S. Paul & Co. Copyrighted 1914; 11 pages (Librarian series No. 3).

Samuleit, Paul
Das Kinematographie als Volks-und Jugendbildungsmittel. Vortrag. Berlin; copyrighted 1912; 60 pages.

Schultze, Ernst
Der Kinematograph als Bildungsmittel. Eine kulturpolitische Untersuchung. Halle a. S. 1911; 158 pages.

Sellmann, Adolf Wilhelm (1868)
Der Kinematograph als Volkserzieher. (Vortrage.)
Langensalzar, H. Beyer & Sohne. Copyrighted 1912;
32 pages. (Padagogisches Magazin. Heft 470.)

Stockton, Rev. E. Boudinot, compiler
Moving pictures suitable for educational purposes; catalogue
for the year 1914. New York, Moving Picture World,
1915. Compiled annually by the Moving Picture World.

Talbot, Frederick A.
Practical Cinematography and Its Applications. London,
W. Heinemann. Copyrighted 1913; 262 pages.

Urban, Charles
The Cinematograph in Science, Education and Matters
of State. London, C. Urban Trading Co. , Ltd. Copyrighted 1907; 56 pages.

Film Making

Hugon, Paul Desmaines
Hints to the Newsfilm Cameraman. Jersey City, Pathe
News. Copyrighted 1915; 16 pages.

Jenkins, C. F.
Picture Ribbons-An exposition of the methods and apparatus employed in the manufacture of the picture ribbons
used in projecting lanterns to give the appearance of
objects in motion. Washington, D. C. The Author,
1897. 57 pages.

Lomas, H. M.
Picture Play Photography. London, Ganes, Ltd. Copyrighted 1914; 269 pages; illustrated.

History of Motion Pictures

Bennett, Colin N.
The Handbook of Kinematography-The history, theory
and practice of motion photography and projection. London, Kinematograph Weekly. 1911. 271 pages; illustrated.

Demeny, Georges
Les Origines du Cinematographie. Paris, H. Paulin &

Cie. Copyrighted 1909; 63 pages.

Liesegang, F. Paul
Die Kinematographic vor 25 Jahren. Mounted clippings
from the Photographische Industrie, 1913. Dusseldorff,
1913.

Motion Pictures-Jurisprudence

Bertram, Alfred
Der Kinematograph in seinen Beziehugen zum Urheber-
recht. Munchen, Duncker und Humblot. Copyrighted
1914; 70 pages.

Cohn, Georg
Kinematographenrecht. Vortrag-Berlin, R. von Becker.
Copyrighted 1909; 48 pages.

Hellwig, Albert Ernst Karl Max (1880)
Rechtquellen des offentlichen Kinematographischenrechts;
systematische Zusammenstellung der wichtigsten deutschen
und fremdem Gesetze und Gesezentwurfe, Ministerialer-
lasse, Polizeiverornungen. M. Gladbach. Copyrighted
1913; 256 pages. (Lichtbuhnen-Bibliothek. Nr. 5.)

Jones, Bernard E.
How to Make and Operate Moving Pictures. A complete
guide to the taking and projecting of cinematograph pictures. New York. Funk & Wagnalls Co. Copyrighted
1916; 216 pages; illustrated.

Juvenile Protective Association of Chicago
Suggestions for regulations of moving pictures. Chicago,
1913.

Kress, E.
Pour ouvirir un cinema. (Formaltites administratives.)
Paris, C. Mendell (Bibliotheque generale de cinematogra-
phie). Copyrighted 1914; 32 pages.

Massachusetts-Statutes
Laws and regulations relating to moving pictures, 1909.
Boston, Wright & Potter Printing Co. 28 pages.

May, Bruno
Das Recht des Kinematographen. Berlin, R. Falk. Copyrighted 1912; 201 pages.

Michigan-Statutes
  Fire marshal law as amended and moving picture show
  law as enacted by the Legislature of 1913. Lansing,
  1913.

Pennsylvania-Statutes
  An act to regulate the construction, maintenance, and
  inspection of buildings used for the exhibition of moving
  pictures, in all cities of the first class, providing for
  the enforcement thereof, and fixing penalties for violations of same.

Texas-Insurance Board
  Moving picture machine booths. Regulations for construction and equipment. Advisory. 1912. Typewritten
  copy.

Von W. Warstal und F. Bergmann
  Kino und Gemeinde. (Die Bedeutung des Gemeindekinos
  fur die Reform des Kinematographenwesens, von W. Warstal. Das Kinowesen von verwaltungsrechtlichen und
  wirtschaflichen Standpunkte, von F. Bergmann.) Lichtbuhnen-Bibliothek. Munchen Nr. 3. Copyrighted 1913;
  112 pages.

Werth, Hans
  Oeffentliches Kinematographen-Recht. Hannover, H.
  Holtje. Copyrighted 1910; 58 pages. Dissertation, Uni-
  versity of Erlangen.

Manufacturers of Motion Pictures

Lists of the manufacturers will be found in the books on
photoplay writing.

Music for Motion Pictures

Ahern, Eugene A.
  What and How to Play for Pictures. Twin Falls, Ind.
  News print. Copyrighted 1913; 61 pages.

True, Lyle C.
  How and What to Play for Moving Pictures. A manual
  and guide for pianists. San Francisco, Music Supply
  Co. Copyrighted 1914; 24 pages.

Photoplays and Photoplay Writing

Adams, Frank Harrington (1890)
The Photoplay Plot. How to write it, how to sell it;
a complete course in motion picture play writing, with
selling advice and an up-to-date list of buyers. Fostoria,
O. United Play Brokerage. Copyrighted 1912; 36 pages.

Arnold, Clyde Nelson
How to Write Scenarios for Photoplays. Complete in-
struction. Youngstown, O. Seena Co. Copyrighted
1914; 20 pages.

Ball, Eustace Hale
The Art of the Photoplay. An elementary text on the
writing of scenarios. Contains sample scenario in text.
New York. Veritas Publishing Co. Copyrighted 1913;
121 pages.
Photoplay Scenarios. How to write and sell them. New
York. Hearst's International Library Co. Copyrighted
1915; 186 pages.

Barker, Ellen Frye
Successful Photoplay Writing. A model play, "Love's
Triumph" (10 typewritten sheets), laid in. A very brief
article. New York. Frye Publishing Co. Copyrighted
1914; 15 pages.

Barker, Ellen Frye
Where to Sell Your Manuscripts. New York. Frye
Publishing Co. Copyrighted 1915; 62 pages.

Caine, Clarence J.
How to Write Photoplays. A reproduction of a series of
articles on the subject as they appeared in the "Hints
for Scenario Writers" department of Picture-Play Weekly
and Picture-Play Magazine. Philadelphia. D. McKay.
Copyrighted 1915; 269 pages.

Carr, Catherine
The Art of Photoplay Writing. Sample scenarios in text.
New York. Hannis. Jordon Co. Copyrighted 1914;
119 pages.

Carter, William and Steele, J. L.
The Photoplay Writer. Cincinnati. Technique Publishing
Co. Copyrighted 1915; 66 pages.

Dench, Ernest A.
  Playwriting for the Cinema. Dealing with the writing
  and marketing of scenarios. London. A. and C. Black.
  Copyrighted 1914; 96 pages.

Dimick, Howard T.
  Photoplay Making. A handbook devoted to the application
  of dramatic principles to the writing of plays for picture
  production. Ridgewood, N. J. Editor Co. Copyrighted
  1915; 103 pages.

Esenwein, Joseph Berg, and Leeds, A.
  Writing the Photoplay. An excellent manual, well writ-
  ten. Model scenarios in text. Springfield, Mass. Home
  Correspondence School. Copyrighted 1913; 374 pages.

Fantus, Felix
  How to Write a Moving Picture Play. Chicago. E. L.
  Fantus Co. Copyrighted 1913; 24 pages.

Gordon, William Lewis
  How to Write Moving Picture Plays. Cincinnati, O.
  Atlas Publishing Co. Copyrighted 1913; two model enve-
  lopes inserted.

Kasai, Chris Kikuzo (1899)
  Instructions on Photoplay Writing. Everett, Wash. Everett Printing Shop. Copyrighted 1915; 16 pages.

Kinobuch, Das
  Kinodramen von Bermann, Hasenclaver, Langer, Lasker-
  Schuler, Keller and others. Leipzig. K. Wolff. Copy-
  righted 1914; 162 pages.

Kleinhaus, Lindley
  The Art of Writing Photoplays. Suggestions to the be-
  ginner. Brooklyn, N. Y. Home Studies Publishing Co.
  Copyrighted 1913; 19 pages.

Liddy, Lewis Wagener
  Photoplay Instructions. Embracing the technical features
  of the photoplay. San Francisco. Western Photoplay
  Association. Copyrighted 1913; 46 pages.

May, Frederick James (1871)
  How to Write a Scenario for a Motion Picture Play.
  Washington. National Scenario Bureau. Copyrighted
  1911; 23 pages.

Mikaloff, Sigurd Gustave, and Schwartz, W. G.
The Rudiments of Photoplay Construction. A complete
course in photoplay writing in book form. McKeesport,
Pa. Commercial Printing Co. Copyrighted 1913; 47
pages.

Moore, Lulu Elizabeth
Key for the Author. A booklet explaining sale and pro-
tection for the photoplay writer. Mattoon, Ill. Com.
Star Co. Copyrighted 1913; 27 pages.

Nelson, John Arthur
The Photoplay; How to Write; How to Sell. Being a
practical and complete treatise upon the form, structure
and technique of the modern motion picture play, together
with an analytical comparison of contra-literary forms
and structures, an investigation of themes and sources.
Suggestions covering how to sell to the best advantage.
Inserted between pages 244-245, "The Lure of the Rose"
a facsimile typewritten photoplay model. Los Angeles.
Photoplay Publishing Co. Copyrighted 1913; 232 pages;
2nd edition.

Newman, Raymond Webster (1892)
Hints and Suggestions Regarding Photoplay Writing. Sample scenario pages 23-31. Washington. Columbia Publishing Co. Copyrighted 1914; 31 pages.

Parsons, Louella O.
How to Write for the "Movies." Chicago. A. C. Mc-
Clurg & Co. Copyrighted 1915; 202 pages.

Pathe Freres
Descriptions of Moving Picture Films. Contents: "Assas-
sination of the Duke of Guise," "The Hunter's Grief,"
"Incriminating Evidence," "The Kiss of Judas," "The
Return of Ulysses," "La Tosca." New York. Copy-
righted 1909; 7 pamphlets; oblong.

Paul, Peter
Das Filmbuch. Wie schreibe ich einen Film und wie
machen ich ihrer zu Geld? Mit 7 Meisterfilms und
einem Kino-Addressbuch. Berlin. W. Borggraber.
Copyrighted 1914; 181 pages.

Phillips, Henry Albert
The Photodrama. The philosophy of its principles, the
nature of its plot, its dramatic construction and technique

illumined by copious examples, together with a complete photoplay and a glossary. Introduction by J. Stuart Blackton (vice-president of the Vitagraph Co.). Larchmont, N. Y. Stanhope-Dodge Publishing Co. Copyrighted 1914; 221 pages. (Authors' handbook series.)

Radnor, Leona
The Photoplay Writer. New York. L. Radnor. Copyrighted 1913; 30 pages; 2nd edition.

Ross, Ernest Nathaniel (1878)
Scenario Writing. Philadelphia. Pennsylvania Association. Copyrighted 1912; 90 pages.

Russell, L. Case
The Photo-Playwright's Primer. Brooklyn. Moving Picture Publishing Co. Copyrighted 1915; 63 pages.

Sargent, Epes Winthrop
The Technique of the Photoplay. New York. Moving Picture World. Copyrighted 1913; 182 pages; 2nd edition.

Slevin, James
On Picture-Play Writing. A handbook of workmanship. Cedar Grove, N. J. Farmer Smith, Inc. Copyrighted 1912; 92 pages.

Thomas, A. W.
How to Write a Photoplay. Preface by B. P. Schulberg of the Famous Players. "This book is not written on a hypothesis, but on the correct standards of forms, covering the field for which it is intended-photoplay production."- Introd. Chicago. Photoplaywrights' Association of America. Copyrighted 1914; 327 pages.

Willhoit, Harry Holdredge (1884), and Yates, W. A.
Complete Course in Photoplay and Short Story Writing. Washington. Griffin Publishing Company. Copyrighted 1915; 26 pages.

Wright, William Lord
The Motion Picture Story. A textbook of photoplay writing. Fergus Falls, Minn. Lundeen Publishing Co. Copyrighted 1915; 227 pages. Sample scenarios in text.

Zuver, Embrie
How to Write Photoplays. Sample scenario, "Timid Teddy." New York. E-Z Scenario Co. Copyrighted

1915; xiv leaves.
Photoplay Writing. Copyrighted 1914.

Projection and Operation

Barber, James W.
The Motor Generator; in Theory and in Practice. London, Ganes, Ltd. Copyrighted 1914; 64 pages; 2nd edition; illustrated.

Bennett, Colin N.
The Handbook of Kinematography. The history, theory and practical motion photography and projection. London. Kinematograph Weekly. 1911; 271 pages; illustrated.

Drum, Harry Chamberlin
Business Policies and Operation Methods for World Film Corporation. New York. McConnell Printing Co. Copyrighted 1915; 120 leaves.

Frippet, E.
La pratique de la photographie instantanee par les appareils à main avec methodes sur les agrandissements et les projections et notes sur le cinematographie. Paris. J. Fritisch. Copyrighted 1899; 219 pages.

Hallberg, J. H.
Hallberg's Catalogue (theatrical supplies). New York. Motion Picture Electricity. New York. Moving Picture World. Copyrighted 1914; 229 pages; illustrated; diagrams.

Horstmann, Henry Charles, and Tousley, V. H.
Motion Picture Operation, Stage Electrics and Illusions. A practical handbook and guide for theater electricians, motion picture operators and managers of theaters and productions. Chicago. F. J. Draka & Co. Copyrighted 1914; 393 pages; illustrated.

Hulfish, David Sherrill
Cyclopedia of Motion Picture Work. A general reference book on the optical lantern, motion head, talking pictures, color motography, specific projecting machines. Chicago. American Technical Society. Copyrighted 1911; 2 volumes; illustrated with over 300 engravings.

Jones, Bernard E.
  The Cinematograph Book.   A complete practical guide to
  the taking and projecting of cinematograph pictures.
  London.   Cassell & Co., Ltd.   Copyrighted 1915;   216
  pages; illustrated.
  How to Make and Operate Moving Pictures.   A complete
  guide to the taking and projecting of cinematograph pictures.   New York.   Funk & Wagnalls Co.   Copyrighted
  1916; 216 pages; illustrated.

Loebel, Leopold
  Le Technique Cinematographie.   Projection, fabbrication
  des films.   Paris.   Copyrighted 1912; 324 pages; illustrated.

Marbe, Karl
  Theorie der kinematographischen Projektionen.   Leipzig.
  Copyrighted 1910; 80 pages; illustrated.

Modern Bioscope Operator, The
  London.   Ganes, Ltd.   Copyrighted 1913; 166 pages; 3rd
  edition.

Rathbun, John B.
  Motion Picture Making and Exhibiting.   A comprehensive
  volume treating the principles of motography, the making
  of motion pictures, the scenario; the motion picture
  theater, the projector; the conduct of film exhibiting;
  methods of coloring films; talking pictures, etc.   Chicago.   C. C. Thompson Co.   Copyrighted 1914; 236
  pages; illustrated.

Richardson, Frank Herbert
  Motion Picture Handbook.   Guide for managers and operators of motion picture theaters.   New York.   Moving
  Picture World.   Copyrighted 1912; 423 pages; illustrated;
  2nd edition; 3rd edition 1916.   702 pages.

Talbot, Frederick A.
  Moving Pictures; How They Are Made and Worked.   Philadelphia.   J. B. Lippincott Co.   Copyrighted 1912; 340
  pages; illustrated.   (Conquest of science.)

Motion Picture Theaters and Exhibitors

The American Motion Picture Directory.   A cyclopedic directory of the motion picture industry, 1914-15.   Chicago.
  American Motion Picture Directory Co.   Copyrighted 1915.

American School of Correspondence.
>   Motion Head. Parts 1-3. Instruction papers prepared
>   by David S. Hulfish. Chicago. The School. Copyrighted
>   1911; 3 volumes.
>   Motion Picture Theaters. Instruction papers. Chicago.
>   The School. 46 pages; illustrated.

Bartholomew, Robert D.
>   Report of the Censorship of Motion Pictures and of In-
>   vestigation of Motion Picture Theaters of Cleveland, 1913.
>   Cleveland, 1913; 32 pages.

Foster, William Trufant (1879)
>   Vaudeville and Motion Picture Shows. A study of theaters
>   in Portland, Oregon. Portland, Ore. Reed College,
>   1914; 63 pages.

Grau, Robert (1858)
>   The Theater of Science. A volume of progress and
>   achievement in the motion picture industry. New York.
>   Broadway Publishing Co. Copyrighted 1914; 378 pages.

Harding, Frank
>   How to Increase Box-Office Receipts. As men of success-
>   ful experience see it. On cover, "The Movie Man's
>   Friend." Grinnell, Ia. Grinnell Herald. Copyrighted
>   1915. 47 pages.

Hill's Gus
>   National Theatrical Directory. Containing the most com-
>   plete list of theaters-moving picture houses. 1914-1915.
>   New York. Hill's National Theatrical Directory. Copy-
>   righted 1914; to be issued annually.

Hodges, James Floyd
>   Opening and Operating Motion Picture Theaters. How
>   it is done successfully. New York. Scenario Publishing
>   Co. Copyrighted 1912; 46 pages; plates; illustrated.
>   Cover title, "Picture Theater Facts."

Kress, E.
>   Comment on Installe et Administre in Cinema. Paris,
>   1914; illustrated; tables. (Bibliotheque de cinematogra-
>   phie.)

Meloy, Arthur S.
>   Theaters and Motion Picture Houses. A practical treatise
>   on the proper planning and construction of such buildings

and containing useful suggestions, rules and data for the
benefits of the architects, prospective owners. New
York. Architects' Supply & Publishing Co. Copyrighted
1916; 121 pages; illustrated; plans and plates.

Michigan-Statutes
Fire marshal law as amended and moving picture show
law as enacted by the Legislature of 1913. (Lansing,
1913.)

Pennsylvania-Statutes
An act to regulate the construction, maintenance and inspection of buildings used for the exhibition of moving
pictures, in all cities of the first class, providing for
the enforcement thereof, and fixing penalties for violations
of same. June 9, 1911.

Rathbun, John B.
Motion Picture Making and Exhibiting. A comprehensive
volume treating the principles of motography, the making
of motion pictures, the scenario, the motion picture
theater, the projector, the conduct of film exhibiting,
methods of coloring films, talking pictures, etc. Chicago. C. C. Thompson Co. Copyrighted 1914; 236
pages; illustrated.

Richardson, Frank Herbert
Motion Picture Handbook. A guide for managers and
operators of motion picture theaters. New York. Moving Picture World. Copyrighted 1912; 423 pages; illustrated. 2nd edition. 3rd edition 1916, 702 pages.

Sargent, Epes Winthrop
Picture Theater Advertising. New York. Moving Picture World. Copyrighted 1915; 302 pages; illustrated.

Schleipmann, Hans
Lichtspeiltheater. Eine Sammlung ausgefuhrter Kino-
hausen in Gross-Berlin. 109 Abbildungen mit Text.
Berlin, 1914; 104 pages.

Texas-Insurance Board
Moving Picture Machine Booths. Regulations for construction and equipment. Advisory, 1912; folio; typewritten copy.

Travellers Insurance Co., Hartford, Conn.
Safety in Moving Picture Theaters. Hartford. Copy-

righted 1914; 40 pages; illustrated.

Warren, Low
The Showman's Advertising Book. Containing hundreds
of money-making tips and wrinkles. Special poster de-
signs by John Hassall and Will Owen. London. E. T.
Herron & Co. Copyrighted 1914; 149 pages; illustrated.

Miscellaneous

Altenloh, Emilie
Zur Soziologie des Kino; die Kino-Unternehumung und
die sozialen Schichten ihrer Besucher. Jena. E.
Diederichs. Copyrighted 1914; 102 pages. (Schriften
zur Soziologie der Kultur.)

Forch, Karl
Der Kinematograph und das sich bewegende Bild; Ge-
schichte und technische Entwicklung der Kinematigraphie
bis zur Gegenwart. Wien. A. Hartleben. Copyrighted
1913; 240 pages; illustrated.

Haefker, Hermann
Kino und Kunst. M. Gladbach. Copyrighted 1913; 71
pages; (Lichtbuhnen-Bibliothek. Nr. 2.)

Hellwig, Albert
Schundfilms; Ihr Wesen, Ihre Gefahren und Ihre Bekamp-
fung. Halle a. d. S. Copyrighted 1911; 139 pages.

Lehman, Hans
Die Kinematographie; Ihre Grundlagen und Ihre Anwen-
dungen. Leipzig. B. G. Teubner. Copyrighted 1911;
117 pages. (Aus Natur und Geisteswelt. Bandchen.
358.)

Liesegang, F. Paul
Lichtbild-und Kino. Technik. M. Gladbach. Copyrighted
1913; 73 pages; illustrated. (Lichtbuhnen-Bibliothek. Nr.
1.)

Lindsay, Nicholas Vachel (1897)
The Art of Moving Pictures. A poet's point of view of
moving pictures. "This book is primarily for photoplay
audiences."- Introduction. New York. Macmillan Co.
Copyrighted 1915; 289 pages.

Manasse, Fritz
Die rechtlichen Grundlagen der Theater--und Kinemato-
graphen--Zensur. Greifswald. J. Abel. Copyrighted
1913; 89 pages. Dissertation, University of Greifswald.

Perlmann, Emil
Der Kulterwelt des Kinematographen. Dusseldorff. Copyrighted 1909; 16 pages.

Potu, E.
La protection internationale des oeuvres cinematogra-
phiques d'apres la convention de Berne, revisee a Berlin
en 1908. Paris. Gauthier-Villars. Copyrighted 1912;
89 pages. (Bibliotheque photographique.)

Vitagraph Company of America
Vitagraph Life Portrayals. How and where pictures are
made by the Vitagraph Company of America. Brooklyn.
Issued by the Publicity Department. Copyrighted 1912;
24 pages; illustrated. Edited by S. M. Spedon.

White, Joseph James
Moviegrins. Chicago. Howells Co. Copyrighted 1915;
56 pages.

Wolf-Czapek, K. W.
Die Kinematographie: Wesen, Entstehung und Ziele des
lebends Bildes. Dresden. Copyrighted 1908; 120 pages;
illustrated.

13. FILM HISTORY CAN ALSO BE FUN

The title of my last chapter may seem somewhat questionable for a work of what I hope will be considered film scholarship. But I could find no other way of introducing some of the more amusing and entertaining aspects of American film history prior to 1920, and so I make no apologies for this chapter. If nothing else, it should prove that one can not only get a sense of achievement from researching a particular period of cinema history, but can also have a good time into the bargain. Somehow I do not imagine this is something which is likely to be true for, say, a classical Greek scholar.

Page after page of early trade periodicals is filled with the most unbelievable nonsense. A typical example is a piece under the heading of "Anarchist Uses Motion Pictures," in the October 13, 1906 issue of Views and Film Index: "At the Palace de Racconigi, a man recently applied for permission to entertain King Victor Emmanual of Italy with motion pictures. Permission was granted and the King shook the man's hand, congratulating him on the quality of the pictures. After he had left it was found that he was Dutto, the anarchist, and the police immediately set upon his track. It is not known why he did not attempt violence, but nevertheless the King recompensed him for an enjoyable picture show."

Anarchy again raised its--to some--ugly head in The Moving Picture World of October 1, 1910, when it was revealed, "The Russian Government, always on the lookout for Nihilists, Anarchists and Socialists, recently placed the Selig Polyscope Company in a bad predicament by seizing the well-known trademark of the S in a diamond. The Selig Polyscope Company mailed to their European agents a number of small electros of their trademark, and when they reached the Russian border, they were seized by the zealous officers, who imagined that these innocent electros were socialistic emblems, sent by the United States to a new revolutionist organization. ...

If Mr. Selig is guilty of anything, it is in trying to educate
and elevate the nations by means of decent, clean and moral
motion pictures."

The behavior of the Russian government was always
good for a laugh--to anyone living outside of the country,
that was, and is. "The Russian government," reported
Variety on September 19, 1913, "has drawn up decrees to
be observed in all picture houses when the Czar and Imperial
Family are included in films. The pictures must be sub-
mitted to the chief of the Emperor's household before being
shown to the public; no music to be played while the film is
being exposed. It must be separate from all other films,
and mentioned on the program as special, the curtain being
lowered before and after the imperial films pass on the screen."

The Russian Royal Family's attitude towards the cinema was not far removed from that of its British cousins.
When Lady Diana Manners appeared in a film, performing
a dance in the manner and the costume of Isadora Duncan,
Queen Mary was reported by Variety (September 26, 1913)
to have uttered "a short, shrill exclamation of surprise,"
and promptly ordered the film destroyed.

Presumably Queen Mary became more blasé about
what might be portrayed in the movies, although it appears
to have taken her a number of years to be able to relax at
a film screening. When she attended a showing of Kalem's
1912 production of From the Manger to the Cross in 1938,
R. Henderson Bland, who portrayed the Christ in the film,
reported, "The seal was put on the delightful informality of
everything by a lady-in-waiting coming over and offering the
Queen a cigarette, which she smoked."

Carl Laemmle at Universal could always be relied
upon for entertainment in the 'teens. It might be through
one of his flamboyant publicity stunts, such as a 1914 cam-
paign to have theatre owners purchase a bale of cotton to
ease the conomic crisis in the South, or his weekly advertisements in The Moving Picture World as part of his fight
against the Motion Picture Patents Company.

On April 17, 1909, Laemmle announced, in a two-
page advertisement, "I have quit the Patents Company. No
more licenses! No more heartbreaks!" This was followed,
week after week, by advertisements with such comments as
"Good Morrow! Have you paid $2.00 for a license to pick
your teeth this week!" or "My country 'tis of thee, sweet

land of liberty, of thee I sing.   Ever heard that before?"
With the advertising revenue that Carl Laemmle brought to
The Moving Picture World, it was not surprising that the
periodical, by May 22, 1909, was describing him as "the
Greatest Film Renter in the World."

It was Carl Laemmle who, in The Universal Weekly
of June 6, 1914, announced that long features were doomed,
and that what the public wanted were two-reelers.   We, of
course, know better now, but Laemmle was not alone in his
assumption.   On April 11, 1914, Epes Winthrop Sargent wrote
in The Moving Picture World, "We do not believe that there
will ever come a time when the one-reel subjects will not
be in demand."   A year previous, on April 9, 1913, W.
Stephen Bush had written glowingly on "The Future of the
Single Reel."

Looking back at these times, it is hard not to be
amused by some of the statements from leaders of the industry.   S. S. Hutchinson of the American Flying A Company
was asked by The Cinema, in its issue of July 9, 1914, if
he thought the talking picture had any future.   "No, I do
not," he replied.   "I can only tell you that if I were offered
the exclusive rights for the world of a perfect speaking picture at a very reasonable price I wouldn't take it."   What
Hutchinson did believe the cinema needed was color.   "It's
worth anything--any sum you like to mention," he added.

Siegmund Lubin foresaw a future for the motion picture which might have become a reality had not television
appeared on the scene.   In Views and Film Index of July 28,
1906, he stated, "I believe the time will come when the live
moving picture machine will be a part and parcel of every
up-to-date home.   I believe that the day is not far distant
when the moving picture film will be delivered at the home
as is the morning newspaper of today and that the written
description of the events of the day before will be augmented
by the realistic portrayal of the happening ....   The day of
actuality is near at hand."

In the June 12, 1909 edition of The Moving Picture
World, the Essanay Company's George K. Spoor envisioned
the film becoming an art form.   "As an art the motion picture will take its place equally with the other arts, and the
epigram quoted in the instance of painting can be said of
motion picture photography as well: 'All passes; Art alone
endures.'"   However, because of the nature of nitrate film,
many early productions, and the art contained therein, were

not to endure.   But it was not through a lack of interest.
As early as 1915, the trade periodical Motography was discussing the need for film preservation.

It was not left entirely to the studio heads to pontif-
icate on the motion picture.   The Moving Picture World
could also be relied upon to pass judgment.   In an article
titled "The Overproduction of Western Pictures," an article
which seems far removed from the Seventies and Sam Peckin-
pah, W. Stephen Bush in The Moving Picture World of October 21, 1911, wrote: "The Western picture seems a con-
stant temptation to 'realism' of a most undesirable variety.
In their natural eagerness to give the public something new,
a never-ending assortment of fresh thrillers and sensational
episodes, the manufacturers dealing in the speciality give
us too close views of 'hold-ups,' hangings, lynchings, mas-
sacres and hair-raising, blood-curdling horrors generally ....
It is the one weak spot in the industry today, the only point
successfully inviting attack from outsiders.   There is no
demand for these pictures.   The field has been thoroughly
exhausted."   I wonder if Bush was aware of the Westerns
that Thomas H. Ince was just beginning to produce for the
New York Motion Picture Company in California?

In 1913, The Moving Picture World was again concerned with realism in films, in particular so-called "Red-
Light" productions.   Louis Reeves Harrison, on October 11,
wrote, "Does not the demand for rotten realism in the drama
come from those of inferior starting point and faulty education
who liken the whole world to themselves."

Diligent research in the trade papers of the period
reveals many fascinating aspects of film history.   Who today
would know that on Friday, April 8, 1910, the Selig Company
in Chicago filmed a hundred-foot film of Enrico Caruso.   The
short was never released, but was intended to be preserved
by Colonel Selig as a valuable souvenir of the great opera
singer's visit to his studios.   Sports fans are doubtless unaware that on May 22, 1915, Madison Square Garden in New
York became a film theatre, opening with the Lubin production
of The Sporting Duchess, starring Rose Coghlan and Ethel
Clayton.   The Moving Picture World of May 29, 1915 reported, "The immense arena, that has been the scene of the
greatest triumphs for Barnum and Bailey's Circus, has been
transformed into seating accommodations for twelve thousand
people, and the selection of Lubin's The Sporting Duchess as
the opening attraction is particularly appropriate, owing to
the magnitude of the production and the subject of the play.

Madison Square Garden has always been the home of the
higher sports, and this play with its atmosphere of the race
course, horseshow, and the sporting pastimes of the smart
set is a fitting feature to inaugurate its opening as a motion
picture theatre. "

Home movies most certainly are nothing new. As far
back as October of 1901, Siegmund Lubin was advertising
the Cineograph, operated, most dangerously it would appear,
by a rubber hose attached to the gas burner. Families visited Lubin's studio at 21 South Eighth Street in Philadelphia
to be filmed, and twenty-four hours later the completed production was ready for viewing in the lucky family's home.

It was the Lubin Company which offered one of the
first racial slurs in the motion picture. The film was Woman's Vanity, released on October 6, 1910, and here is the
description from The Moving Picture World of October 8,
1910: "The very latest thing in dresses is worn by an exceptionally pretty girl who attracts more attention than she
bargained for and throws the dress away. It falls into the
hands of a negress who is followed by the same crowd of
men who trailed the heiress. Then they found out her color. "
This same gag, with variations, was to be used by both Mack
Sennett and Hal Roach through the Thirties.

One of the most famous of Indian defeats, The Battle
at Wounded Knee, was filmed by the Essanay Company in
1913, with the participation of Buffalo Bill Cody and the Sioux
Indians of the Pine Ridge Reservation in South Dakota. It
was directed by Vernon Day and Theodore Wharton, and much
has been written about it, in particular that a print was deposited by the Essanay Company in the National Archives.
In fact, the film was not released until 1917, when, because
of the publicity surrounding the death of Cody, it was re-
titled The Life of Buffalo Bill and the Indian Wars. No print
was deposited with the National Archives, because the National
Archives was not established until 1934. Prints were given
to the War Department and the Department of the Interior,
but no such prints had survived until the National Archives
came into being.

All too few company records have survived from the
cinema's infancy, but those that have contain not only much
that is valuable to researchers, but also much that is highly
entertaining and amusing. I particularly delight in a note,
by an unknown hand, in the files of the Edison Company, in
which Albert E. Smith of the Vitagraph Company is quoted as

saying, "Rotten as Lubin pictures are, Edison are worse."
Rotten also, according to William McChesney of the Edison
Company, was the footage shot of opera star Anna Case in
September of 1916. Suggesting that this short, titled Anna
Case, the Prettiest Girl in Grand Opera, be drastically
edited, McChesney commented, "She certainly succeeded in
making a dunce of herself by her attempt to act. I suggested
that all of her grimaces be cut out and that we leave in only
those parts which show her comparatively unconscious of the
fact that she is being photographed."

The papers of Colonel William N. Selig, housed in
the Margaret Merrick Library of the Academy of Motion
Picture Arts and Sciences, reveal two delightful letters, both
of which are well worth reprinting almost in their entirety.
They both indicate the problems which early film producers
came up against.

The first is from the Atchison, Topeka and Santa Fe
Railway System, and is dated December 9, 1913:

"Some time ago a report reached this office to the
effect that one of your photoplays, entitled The Only Chance,
was being exhibited throughout the West and that this play
showed the Santa Fe up in rather a bad light. The scene is
located somewhere along the Santa Fe, presumably in Arizona,
as much of the equipment bore the name of our S. F. P. & P.
lines. The story, I understand, has to do with a case of
carelessness on the part of an operator, or that the operator
has been overworked and had gone to sleep at the post. At
any rate, a train passed his station and only by the mirac-
ulous work of the hero was a fearful wreck averted.

"I am sure you will appreciate the feeling of the Santa
Fe operating officials on hearing of such publicity at this
time, when public attention is being centered on such events
as recent wrecks of the New York, New Haven & Hartford,
and when newspapers and legislators are putting in a good
deal of their time considering ways and means of safeguarding
travellers. The Santa Fe is making every effort to safeguard
its trains and we feel that films of this character are harm-
ful.

"In view of these circumstances, I am certain that
this matter, being brought to your attention, will result in
your issuing the necessary instructions to have the name and
trade mark of the Santa Fe and its subsidiary lines painted
out of the film."

The second letter comes from the Department of Police of the city of Detroit, and is dated July 3, 1911:

"In the past few months, this department has had so many complaints in regards to moving picture film posters of an undesirable nature; we have concluded to notify you in regards to same, because the majority of house managers claim inability to understand what we desire and what we object to ....

"We call your attention to the fact that a poster is a stationary picture, that is studied by the passerby, both young and old; consequently making an important asset in the way of advertising, while remembering the fact and giving you the greatest consideration we have to protect the child from the evil seed of crime becoming planted in its youthful brain; that is the reason why, WHAT IS PERMISSIBLE IN A MOVING PICTURE WOULD NEVER DO FOR A STATIONERY PICTURE, WHICH USUALLY RENDERS A WRONG CONCLUSION TO THE MIND.

"We will give as nearly as possible our ideas of what we tolerate and what we object to.

"First, Western Pictures; if the characters are in costume we do not object to the display of firearms. Indians and cowboys fighting are permissible, for it bears on real history.

"Second, Battle Scenes, soldiers in uniforms, with guns, and swords fighting, etc., is permissible.

"Third, Head Pictures, house scenes, Western saloons, etc., are permissible.

"WHAT WE OBJECT TO AND DON'T WANT:

"First, Murders, firebranding buildings, unless it be done by Indians or soldiers. It is a most dangerous of felonious acts.

"Second, Pictures of criminals in prison garb. Prison scenes and escaping convicts.

"Third, Attempts of murder, people tied in chairs, gags in or around peoples' mouths, stabbing, holding people at bay with firearms, scenes of choking, and any other pictures of violent deaths or acts.

"Fourth, Blowing of safes, robberies, or any other unlawful or felonious acts.

"Fifth, Drinking, tottering drunkards, gambling, duelling, inside pictures of houses of prostitution, suggestive pictures and scantily clad women.

"Sixth, Display of black hand letters, strikers, rioters, and any violent destruction of property."

Aside from the illiterate nature of this letter from the Detroit police, what is most amusing and most sad is that the list of objections sounds like a word-picture of downtown Detroit today.

The whole field of film posters is in need of study. There are many books of film posters, all pretty to look at but offering nothing solid in terms of research or scholarship. I have nothing to offer here, except an amusing story told me by Adolph Zukor's son, Eugene. Most film posters from the 'teens were lithographed by the Miner Company of Cleveland, whose owner, Walter Moore, would often come to New York to discuss business with his various clients. Moore was always upset that he could never meet with the industry leaders at their club, because the industry leaders were Jewish, their club only admitted Jews, and Moore was a Protestant. Rather than have Walter Moore change his religion, a special resolution was passed by the club in question to admit him to membership.

In any decade, the change of name by an actor or actress can often cause merriment. Who would believe that Clara Viola Cronk could become the beautiful Claire Windsor, a name change suggested by director Lois Weber? The most famous cognomen change in the 'teens was undoubtedly that of Samuel Goldfish to Samuel Goldwyn, as reported in Variety of January 3, 1919. It was Variety (May 31, 1918) which also revealed that Lila Lee had acted under the name of "Cuddles." (Her real name was Augusta Appel.) Director Rex Ingram had changed his name from Rex Hitchcock in the mid 'teens, a switch which, I discovered on a visit to Ireland some years ago, led to many of the residents of his hometown believing that their most famous native son was Alfred Hitchcock.

A change in studios might also mean a change in name for some players. When Augustus Carney went from Essanay to Universal, he changed his film name from Alkali Ike to

Universal Ike. The First World War produced other name
changes, the most extraordinary of which was reported in
the fan magazines of October, 1918: Gustav von Seyffertitz
had become G. Butler Clonebaugh for the duration.

A close reading of Variety in the early and mid-'teens
reveals many reviews of vaudeville acts by individuals who
were to gain later screen fame. On May 11, 1917, the paper
took a look at the Duncan Sisters' new act at New York's
Fifth Avenue Theatre, and was not wildly enthusiastic: "....
a stereotyped sister act. The girls possess a restricted
song routine .... The Duncan Sisters are not ripe as yet
for the big time." (Readers wishing a delightful study of
the Duncan Sisters should read Edward Wagenknecht's As
Far as Yesterday, published by the University of Oklahoma
Press in 1968.) A fourteen-minute performance of society
dances by Mae Murray and Clifton Webb came in for much
praise in the March 20, 1914 issue of Variety. Commented
reviewer Mark, "In a becoming pink chartreuse outfit over
chiffon, Miss Murray's pretty arms, hands and feet seemed
set to music. That Palace audience Monday night went plumb
daffy over her dancing. In praising her splendid dancing
Webb should not be overlooked."

Mention of Clifton Webb, whose devotion to his mother
was legendary, brings to mind an earlier actor similarly
besotted. J. Warren Kerrigan was an insipid leading man,
whose appeal in the 'teens is hard to appreciate today. He
almost ruined his career in 1917, by announcing in the Denver
Times of May 11, "I am not going to war until I have to.
I will go, of course, if my country needs me, but I think
that first they should take the great mass of men who aren't
good for anything else, are good only for the lower grades
of work. Actors, musicians, great writers, artists of every
kind--isn't it a pity when people are sacrificed who are capable of such things--of adding to the beauty of the world."
He was immediately attacked by Photoplay which, in an editorial in August of 1917, dubbed him one of the beautiful
slackers.

The subtitle is an area of silent films which has received little attention. Admittedly, the films of the 'teens,
D. W. Griffith's productions aside, offer little exciting in
the way of titles. Only in the Twenties did the subtitle become an art form, with such wit as "Fifth Avenue where all
good little minks go when they die" becoming an accepted
part of such program pictures as Colleen Moore's Orchids
and Ermine (1927). Many critics and historians today have

J. Warren Kerrigan

spoken out against the subtitle. I don't agree with them. I am only too aware of how much better, say, F. W. Murnau's The Last Laugh would have been with the help of a few titles. William C. de Mille praised the title, claiming, "the subtitle is not an interruption, but is as important as the Greek chorus. There is much of life that can only be expressed with the aid of words, the psychological overtones and colours, which action alone cannot portray. We will be no more able to dispense with the sub-title in the photoplay than we can eliminate action from the spoken word."

In the 'teens, there were those who disagreed with de Mille. Exhibitor's Trade Review (March 29, 1919) commented, "A sub-title is a necessary evil. Just that--and nothing more. It is our observation that most sub-titles are more evil than necessary. Many pictures leave nothing to the imagination." There were at least two articles on subtitling: "The Making of Photoplay Titles" by Lawrence Williams in Motion Picture Magazine (March 1919) and "The Illustrated Title" by Ellen D. Tarleaw in Motion Picture Magazine (March 1920).

Certainly, the use of subtitles changed in the 'teens. They no longer told one the action about to be played on the screen by the mid 'teens, as was the case in all of the one-reelers. I recall presenting a program on Thomas Ince, and after one of his early productions had been screened, a film director turned college professor commented on the Brechtian influence in Ince's films, evidenced by the titles appearing before, and explaining, the action. Ridiculous as was his remark, I could not help contemplating how many intellectuals might be willing to concede an Inceian influence in the works of Brecht.

The final word on subtitles must go to Marjorie Charles Driscoll, who summed it all up in a poem, published in Motion Picture Classic:

> I met a very ancient man
> with gray and revered head.
> "It's growing dark," I said to him,
> And this is what he said.
>
> "Drifting shadows crept over the
> world, as suppliant Day knelt at the
> threshold of Night, pleading for the
> boon of darkness."

I looked at him in mild surprise.
He wept: "Ah, well-a-day!
I once wrote titles for the films,
And now I talk this way!"

On more than one occasion villains in real life have
portrayed themselves on the screen. Outlaw Emmett Dalton
played himself in, and also produced, Beyond the Law, released in the winter of 1918 on a state rights basis by the
Southern Feature Film Corporation. The six-reel production
was directed by Theodore Marston and written by William
Addison Lathrop. The Moving Picture World (December 24,
1918) commented, "The production is not one which we will
criticise as a bit of dramatic fiction, nor as a film intended
to meet the highest standards of artistic picture craft. On
the contrary, we view each scene of the picture narrative
with the same eager anticipation of coming events as the
small boy feels for the storybook heroes."

In the April 18, 1914 issue of The Moving Picture
World appeared an advertisement, signed by Emmett Dalton,
stating, "This is to inform you that 'fake' Moving Picture
Films, purporting to represent the lives of the Dalton Boys,
are being shown throughout the country. My brothers' pictures and mine are copyrighted. I will prosecute anyone
(theatre or individual) who shows, impersonates, or attempts
to do same, without my or my mother's consent. Neither
have I any relatives out showing Dalton films ...."

I was responsible for the acquisition and preservation
(in the National Film Collection at the Library of Congress)
of one of the films to which Dalton refers, The Dalton Boys.
The original print contained no information as to the company
responsible for the production. I believe it to be the earliest
extant production concerning the Dalton gang. Emmett Dalton
died--of old age--in Los Angeles in 1937.

Although W. B. "Bat" Masterson, as far as I know,
never appeared in films, he was a great admirer of the work
of William S. Hart. While Hart was appearing at Wallack's
Theatre, New York, in The Squaw Man, Masterson wrote to
him on December 17, 1905: "I received your photo taken in
the picturesque cowboy garb that was once so familiar to me,
and let me assure you that I greatly prize the picture and
thank you sincerely for remembering me, and it is now holding down one of the places of honor on the mantle piece where
it will serve as a reminder of those days on our western
border that have passed into history and made way, as I view

it, for a more unstable and effete civilization. Your portrayal of Cash Hawkins the cowboy desperado is exceptionally good-- giving as you do to the part the proper atmosphere in every detail. "

If "Bat" Masterson, who by the time of this letter had become a real estate agent, considered the New York of 1905 "an unstable and effete civilization," what would he have made of today and Mel Brooks' Blazing Saddles?

To close this chapter, and this book, I would like to reprint a column, "Musings of a Photoplay Philosopher" from the April 1911 issue of The Motion Picture Story Magazine. In one paragraph, it explains the raison d'être for the cinema, and it's an explanation which no one would dare to admit to today.

> Leaving my house last night at seven-
> thirty, I saw one motion picture perfor-
> mance from beginning to end, including
> five plays and two songs, and at nine I
> was back home. My neighbor in the ad-
> joining hallroom left to go to a theater at
> seven-thirty and arrived home at eleven-
> fifteen. He saw one play, I saw five; it
> cost him $1.50, it cost me ten cents;
> nearly four hours of his life are gone,
> only one-and-a-half of mine. The moral
> I draw from this is, that the photoplay
> is in harmony with modern methods and
> progressive civilization. Nearly all of
> our great inventions and discoveries are
> directed toward the elimination of distance
> and the reduction of labor, in order that
> we may save time. We have the four-
> day ocean liners, the eighty-mile-an-hour
> trains, automobiles, airships, telephones,
> wireless telegraphy, and labor-saving
> machinery of every description; and what
> are they all for if not to gain time and
> to save expense?

APPENDICES

The bibliographies presented here are devoted exclusively to the companies themselves, and not to their films or to the personalities connected with them. Thus one will look in vain under the Edison Company for biographies of Thomas Edison, or under the Biograph Company for articles about D. W. Griffith. No claim is made that these bibliographies are in any way definitive, but an effort has been made to note all major articles in important periodicals such as The Moving Picture World.

THE BALBOA COMPANY: A Bibliography

1. "Balboa Continues to Grow," The Moving Picture World (September 4, 1915).

2. "The Balboa Enterprise," The Moving Picture World (July 10, 1915).

3. "Balboa's Plant Growing Steadily," The Moving Picture World (September 23, 1916).

4. "Horkheimer on the Job," The Moving Picture World (January 15, 1916).

5. "Horkheimer to Make Mutual Series," The Moving Picture World (March 17, 1917).

6. "Horkheimer Watches All Details of Production," Motion Picture News (March 20, 1915).

7. "Horkheimer Would Aid Red Cross," The Moving Picture World (December 15, 1917).

8. Peck, Charles Mortimer. "Is the Scenario Writer Worthy

of His Hire?" Motion Picture News (January 9, 1915).

9. "Ruth Roland Goes to Balboa for Three Years," Motion Picture News (December 19, 1914).

10. "The Story of a Studio," Motography (June 16, 1917).

THE BIOGRAPH COMPANY: A Bibliography

1. "Biograph Company Define Their Position," The Moving Picture World (March 14, 1908).

2. "Biograph Kids Are Wonderful Girls," Motography (July 4, 1914).

3. "Biograph vs. Edison," The Moving Picture World (February 29, 1908).

4. "Biograph Western Studios," The Moving Picture World (July 10, 1915).

5. Blaisdell, George. "Quality in Biograph Multiples," The Moving Picture World (December 12, 1914).

6. Bowser, Eileen, ed. Biograph Bulletins, 1908-1912. New York: Octagon Books, 1973.

7. Dickson, W. K. L. The Biograph in Battle. London: T. Unwin Fisher, 1901.

8. Dougherty, Lee E. "Conditions and Features," The Moving Picture World (July 11, 1914).

9. Gatchell, Charles. "The Cradle of the Movies," Picture Play (May, 1917).

10. Griffith, Mrs. D. W. When the Movies Were Young. New York: Dutton, 1925.

11. Hall, Harold R. "Biograph, the Magic Name of the Movies," Motion Picture Classic (June, 1927).

12. Harrison, Louis Reeves. "Studio Saunterings," The Moving Picture World (February 24, 1912).

13. Henderson, Robert M. D. W. Griffith: The Years at Biograph. New York: Farrar, Straus and Giroux, 1970.

14. "Ladies, Please Remove Their Hats," New York Telegram (November 12, 1932).

15. "Lee Dougherty Recalls Early Days," The Moving Picture World (September 23, 1916).

16. Niver, Kemp R. Mary Pickford, Comedienne. Los Angeles: Locare Research Group, 1969.

17. _____, ed. Biograph Bulletins, 1896-1908. Los Angeles: Locare Research Group, 1971.

18. "Old Biograph Coming Back?" Motion Picture News (September 4, 1920).

19. Stern, Seymour. "11 East 14th Street," Films in Review (October, 1952).

20. "Ten Year Old Comedy Reminiscence," Motion Picture News (November 20, 1920).

21. "Where the 'Biographs' Are Made," Motography (September 20, 1913).

THE EDISON COMPANY: A Bibliography

1. Bush, W. Stephen. "A Chat with Thomas A. Edison," The Moving Picture World (July 11, 1914).

2. Clarke, Charles G. "The Case for the Inventor of Motion Pictures," American Cinematographer (November, 1961).

3. Crosland, Alan. "How Edison's 'Black Maria' Grew," Motography (April 22, 1916).

4. Dickson, Antonia and W. K. L. The Edison Vitascope. Privately printed, 1894.

5. _____. Edison's Invention of the Kineto-Phonograph. Los Angeles: Pueblo Press, 1939.

6. _____ . History of the Kinetograph, Kinetoscope and Kineto-Phonograph. New York: Arno Press, 1970.

7. "Edison and Kleine Combine to Produce Five-Reelers," Motion Picture News (July 31, 1915).

8. "The Edison Banquet," The Moving Picture World (December 31, 1909).

9. "Edison Company's Statement," The Moving Picture World (February 29, 1908).

10. "Edison Company's Position," The Moving Picture World (April 4, 1908).

11. "Edison-McClure," The Moving Picture World (June 29, 1912).

12. "Edison Players Return," The Moving Picture World (November 16, 1912).

13. "Edison Progress," The Moving Picture World (December 11, 1909).

14. "Edisonia," Exhibitors' Times (August 30, 1913).

15. Harrison, Louis Reeves. "Studio Saunterings," The Moving Picture World (April 13, 1912).

16. _____ . "The Edison Talking Machine," The Moving Picture World (March 1, 1913).

17. _____ . "Fire Wrecks Edison Studio," The Moving Picture World (April 11, 1914).

18. Hendricks, Gordon. "A Collection of Edison Films," Image (Number 3, 1959).

19. _____ . The Edison Motion Picture Myth. Berkeley: University of California Press, 1961.

20. _____ . "A New Look at an Old Sneeze," Film Culture (Number 22/23, 1961).

21. _____ . Origins of the American Film. New York: Arno Press, 1972.

22. Hulette, Frank Parker. "An Interview with Thomas A.

Edison," The Moving Picture World (July 22, 1911).

23. "Kleine-Edison Merger Formed," The Moving Picture World (July 24, 1915).

24. "Plympton Back from Europe," The Moving Picture World (April 12, 1913).

25. Ramsaye, Terry. "Edison Whimsy Founded Industry," Motion Picture Herald (October 24, 1931).

26. _____. "A Man for the Ages," Motion Picture Herald (October 24, 1931).

27. _____. "Ten Years from Now--Edison," Photoplay (May, 1922).

28. Spehr, Paul C. "Edison Films at the Library of Congress," The Quarterly Journal of the Library of Congress (January, 1975).

29. Svejda, George J. The Black Maria Site Study. Washington: Office of Archeology and Historical Preservation, 1969.

THE ESSANAY COMPANY: A Bibliography

1. "The 'Acting' Member of Essanay," The Moving Picture World (January 6, 1912).

2. Bushman, Francis X. "From the Inside of the Studio," Picture-Play Weekly (April 10, 1915).

3. "The Essanay Chaplin Comedies," The Moving Picture World (July 10, 1915).

4. "The Essanay Company Out West," The Moving Picture World (December 4, 1909).

5. "The Essanay Company's New Plant," The Moving Picture World (June 5, 1909).

6. "Essanay Reaches R. I. P. in Video," Variety (February 28, 1973).

7. "Essanay Western Plant," The Moving Picture World (July 10, 1915).

8. "Essanay's New Studio," The Moving Picture World (March 4, 1916).

9. "Essanay's New Studios," The Moving Picture World (July 11, 1914).

10. Grisham, William F. "Those Marvellous Men and Their Movie Machines," Chicago Tribune Magazine (December 7, 1969).

11. Holmes, Charles R. "Gilbert M. Anderson Back at Niles Studio," The Moving Picture World (February 13, 1915).

12. "In the Far West," The Bioscope (February 9, 1911).

13. McGuirk, Charles J. "I Knew Them When," Photoplay (March, 1925).

14. McQuade, James S. "Essanay Plant Like a Beehive," The Moving Picture World (December 23, 1916).

15. _____. "Essanay's Western Producer, G. M. Anderson," The Film Index (July 30, 1910).

16. Millstead, Thomas. "The Movie the Indians Almost Won," Westways Magazine (December, 1970).

17. "Natural Vision Goes into Essanay Cutting Room," Exhibitors Herald (January 29, 1927).

18. "New Essanay Stock Company," The Moving Picture World (December 2, 1916).

19. Parsons, Louella O. "The Essanay Days," Theatre Arts (July, 1951).

20. Priddy, Gladys. "Essanay Lot Gone, Not It's Guiding Hand," Chicago Sunday Tribune (December 21, 1947).

21. "Some Prominent Essanay Photoplayers," The Moving Picture World (July 11, 1914).

22. Spoor, George K. "Remarkable Growth of Motion Picture Industry," The Moving Picture World (July 11, 1914).

23. _____ . "The Turning of the Ways," The Moving Picture World (March 10, 1917).

24. Starr, Louis M. "Flickers of the Past Make a Clear Picture to Essanay's Mr. S.," Chicago Sun (February 2, 1947).

25. _____ . "How Chicago Spawned an Industry--and a Lot of Great Names," Chicago Sun (January 26, 1947).

THE KALEM COMPANY: A Bibliography

1. "The Ben Hur Case," The Bioscope (February 22, 1912).

2. "Biblical History Pictured," The Bioscope (May 9, 1912).

3. Blaisdell, George. "Sid Olcott in Traveltalk," The Moving Picture World (January 17, 1914).

4. Bush, W. Stephen. "From the Manger to the Cross," The Moving Picture World (October 26, 1912).

5. _____ . "Samuel Long," The Moving Picture World (August 14, 1915).

6. "A Charming Dare-Devil," Pictures and the Picturegoer (March 13, 1915).

7. Clark, Jack. "Putting on a Picture in Egypt," The Moving Picture World (June 1, 1912).

8. Condon, Mabel. "Hot Chocolate and Reminiscences at Nine of the Morning," Photoplay (January, 1915).

9. Courtlandt, Roberta. "Troubles of the Camera Man," Motion Picture Classic (August, 1916).

10. Denig, Lynde. "The Kalem Viewpoint," The Moving Picture World (August 7, 1915).

11. "Editor Becomes Vice-President," The Moving Picture World (August 21, 1915).

12. Gauntier, Gene. Blazing the Trail. Unpublished manuscript in the files of the Museum of Modern Art, dated December 16, 1928.

13. Harrison, Louis Reeves. "Studio Saunterings," The Moving Picture World (July 6, 1912).

14. "Helen Gibson Replaces Helen Holmes in the Hazards of Helen Railroad Series," Motion Picture News (August 28, 1915).

15. Joyce, Alice. "How I Got In," Motion Picture Magazine (August, 1917).

16. "Kalem Players Combine in Search for Picturesque Locations," Motion Picture News (March 31, 1917).

17. "Kalem Railroad Films Have Seven Years' History," Motion Picture News (January 8, 1916).

18. "Kalem Sends Company to the Orient," The Moving Picture World (December 16, 1911).

19. "Kalem Sends Stock Company to Ireland," The Moving Picture World (June 3, 1911).

20. Mapes, Alice. "A Kalem Girl in Ireland," The Moving Picture World (July 15, 1911).

21. "Marion Optimistic," The Moving Picture World (March 23, 1912).

22. McGowan, J. P. "O'Kalems Return to Ireland," The Moving Picture World (August 10, 1912).

23. Mitchell, George. "Sidney Olcott," Films in Review (April, 1954).

24. Photoplay Arts Portfolio of Kalem Moving Picture Stars. New York: Photoplay Arts, 1914.

25. Slide, Anthony. "The Colleen Bawn," Vision (Spring, 1967).

26. _____. "From the Manger to the Cross," Vision (Summer, 1967).

27. _____. "The Kalem Serial Queens," The Silent Pic-

ture (Winter, 1968).

28. _____. "The O'Kalems," Cinema Studies (September, 1967).

29. "Some Egyptian Pictures," The Bioscope (June 27, 1912).

THE LUBIN COMPANY: A Bibliography

1. "Betzwood Film Company Buys Lubin's Betzwood Plant," The Moving Picture World (February 16, 1918).

2. "Betzwood on the Perkiomen," Motography (August 23, 1913).

3. "Betzwood, the 500-Acre Studio," The New York Dramatic Mirror (March 18, 1914).

4. Brockhouser, Frank. "Philadelphia Was Hollywood before Hollywood," Philadelphia Sunday Bulletin (October 22, 1967).

5. Bush, W. Stephen. "Betzwood, the Great," The Moving Picture World (July 11, 1914).

6. _____. "A Day with Siegmund Lubin," The Moving Picture World (July 11, 1914).

7. "For Nine Years, Betzwood Was Film Capital," Morristown Times Herald (May 23, 1970).

8. "Get Off at Lubin," The Moving Picture World (September 13, 1913).

9. Harrison, Louis Reeves. "Studio Saunterings," The Moving Picture World (March 30, 1912).

10. Headley, Robert K., Jr. "The First Mini-Movie Complex?" Marquee (Volume 4, Number 1, 1972).

11. "In the Field with Hotaling," The Moving Picture World (January 11, 1913).

12. "Lost in Lubin Fire," The Moving Picture World (July 11, 1914).

13. Lubin, Siegmund. "A Toast to Those Who Make Mistakes," The Moving Picture World (March 10, 1917).

14. "Lubin at Jacksonville," The Moving Picture World (February 10, 1912).

15. "Lubin West Coast Plant," The Moving Picture World (July 10, 1915).

16. "Melville's Success with Western Lubin," The Moving Picture World (April 3, 1915).

17. Nixon, Charles E. "Lubin of Lubinville," Movie Pictorial (July, 1915).

18. Pennington, Esther. "On the Inside of Lubinville," Photoplay (February, 1915).

19. "'Pop' Lubin Dies after Long Illness," Motion Picture News (September 22, 1923).

20. Romaine Fielding and the Lubin Moving Picture Company. Santa Fe: New Mexico State Record Center and Archives, 1970.

21. "S. Lubin Buys $100,000 Estate," The Moving Picture World (August 31, 1921).

22. "S. Lubin Philosopher," The Moving Picture World (March 1, 1913).

23. "Savage-Lubin Movie Deal Reported in Consummation," Variety (January 30, 1914).

24. "Sigmund Lubin Talks," Exhibitors' Times (September 27, 1913).

25. "Three Studios in One Plan for Lubin at 20th Street," Motion Picture News (February 19, 1916).

THE PARALTA COMPANY: A Bibliography

1. "Carl Anderson Promises Splendid Plays," The Moving Picture World (April 6, 1918).

2. "Change in Ownership of Paralta," The Moving Picture World (May 25, 1918).

3. "Paralta Engages Raymond B. West," The Moving Picture World (October 6, 1917).

4. "Paralta Plays, Inc. Is New Company," The Moving Picture World (April 7, 1917).

5. "Paralta Quits Triangle," The Moving Picture World (October 6, 1917).

6. "Paralta 'Repeats' to Cost Exhibitors Nothing," Motion Picture News (April 14, 1917).

7. "Work on Paralta Studios Progressing," The Moving Picture World (April 13, 1918).

THE SELIG COMPANY: A Bibliography

1. Aye, John. "Silent Jim Campbell," Photoplay (May, 1916).

2. Bateman, Richard Dale. "The Founding of the Hollywood Motion Picture Industry," Journal of the West (October, 1971).

3. Beall, Harry Hammond. "The Packing House of Canned Drama," The Rounder (October 29, 1910).

4. Blaisdell, George. "Great Selig Enterprise," The Moving Picture World (July 10, 1915).

5. Bosworth, Hobart. "The Picture Forty-Niners," Photoplay (December, 1915).

6. Conlon, "Scoop." "First Movie Studio in California Starts in Old Chinese Laundry," San Francisco Chronicle (January 15, 1922).

7. Cooke, Philip St. George, comp. Tom Mix and the Selig Polyscope Company. Santa Fe: New Mexico State Record Center and Archives, 1970.

8. Dengler, Eugene. "The Wonders of a Picture Factory,"

Motography (July, 1911).

9. Edwards, Leo. "An Afternoon at the Selig Studio," Feature Movie Magazine (April 15, 1915).

10. "A Fortune for Animal Actors," Picture-Play Weekly (April 17, 1915).

11. Henry, Bill. "By the Way," Los Angeles Times (January 31, 1940).

12. "Hunting African Big Game in the Jungles of Chicago," The Moving Picture World (July 31, 1909).

13. "Kleine, Edison, Selig and Essanay in Combination," The Moving Picture World (September 16, 1916).

14. Lahue, Kalton C. Motion Picture Pioneer: The Selig Polyscope Company. New York: A. S. Barnes, 1973.

15. McQuade, James. "Director James Colin Campbell," The Moving Picture World (March 27, 1915).

16. _____. "Famous Cowboys in Motion Pictures," The Film Index (June 25, 1910).

17. _____. "Making Selig Pictures," The Film Index (November 20, 1909).

18. _____. "Twenty-One Years in the Business," The Moving Picture World (May 12, 1917).

19. "Maintaining a Wild Animal Jungle for Pictures," Motography (November 9, 1912).

20. "A Notable Film Producer," The Moving Picture World (June 12, 1909).

21. "Producing Selig Animal Pictures," Picture-Play Weekly (June 5, 1915).

22. Selig, William N. "Cutting Back," Photoplay (February, 1920).

23. "Selig Polyscope Studios in Chicago Opened on 6th," Motion Picture News (March 18, 1916).

24. "Selig Talks," The Film Index (September 18, 1909).

25. "Selig--The Great Moving Picture Plant of the West,"
    The Moving Picture World (August 21, 1909).

26. Shorey, F. N. "Making a Selig Film," The Film Index
    (January 30, 1909).

27. "A Visit to Selig's Jungle Zoo," The New York Dramatic
    Mirror (January 27, 1915).

28. "Wild Beasts in Motion Pictures," The Movie Magazine
    (August, 1915).

29. "William N. Selig Perfects Strong Organization," Motion
    Picture News (July 31, 1915).

30. "World's Most Aristocratic Animal House," Photoplay
    (August, 1915).

THE THANHOUSER COMPANY: A Bibliography

1. Blaisdell, George. "Thanhouser in New Studio," The
   Moving Picture World (January 17, 1914).

2. "Charles J. Hite," Reel Life (August 29, 1914).

3. Darnell, Jean. "Children of the Photoplay," Photoplay
   (December, 1913).

4. "A Day with Thanhouser," The Moving Picture World
   (April 24, 1915).

5. Duncan, Robert C. "Forty-Five Minutes from Broadway,"
   Picture Play (January, 1917).

6. "Edwin Thanhouser Is Back," The Moving Picture World
   (March 6, 1915).

7. Harrison, Louis Reeves. "Studio Saunterings," The
   Moving Picture World (July 13, 1912).

8. Jones, Kenyon. "At the Home of The Million Dollar
   Mystery," Photoplay (October, 1914).

9. Lambert, Glen. "Thanhouser Forces Gather in Jackson-ville, Florida," Motion Picture News (January 22, 1916).

10. Lonergan, Lloyd. "How I Came to Write 'Continuity,'" The Moving Picture World (July 21, 1917).

11. "Mignon Anderson of the Thanhouser Company," Motion Picture Story Magazine (February, 1913).

12. Photoplay Arts Portfolio of Thanhouser Moving-Picture Stars. New York: Photoplay Arts, 1914.

13. Slide, Anthony. "Mignon Anderson," in The Idols of Silence. New York: A. S. Barnes, 1976.

14. _____. "Mignon Anderson Donates Early Film Stills," The Magazine (January-February, 1976).

15. _____. "The Thanhouser Company," Films in Review (November, 1975).

16. Thanhouser, Edwin. "Reminiscences of Picture's Boy-hood Days," The Moving Picture World (March 10, 1917).

17. "Thanhouser Back as Head of New Rochelle Concern," Motion Picture News (March 6, 1915).

18. "Thanhouser Company: A New Film Producer," The Moving Picture World (March 12, 1910).

19. "Thanhouser on Talent Hunt, Bags More Favorites," Motion Picture News (July 10, 1915).

20. "Thanhouser Plant Burns," The Moving Picture World (January 25, 1913).

21. "Those Thanhouser Kids," Photoplay (February, 1915).

22. "Two Noted Directors Acquired by Thanhouser," Motion Picture News (March 31, 1917).

SOURCE MATERIAL ON AMERICAN FILM
PRODUCTION PRIOR TO 1920*

In my researches with the American Film Institute on
early American film production, initially as a Louis B. Mayer
Research Associate and later with preparatory work on The
American Film Institute Catalog: Feature Films 1911-1920,
I have been able to uncover and gain access to more research
material on the American cinema prior to 1920 than most
other people working in the same field. What strikes me
time and again is not that so much contemporary material
is lost, but that so much has survived, and that what has
survived is cataloged in a totally inadequate fashion.

Company records are, quite naturally, the primary--
indeed the most important--source of research. The holdings
of the Museum of Modern Art (11 West 53 Street, New York,
N. Y. 10019) in relation to the American Biograph Company
and D. W. Griffith are well-known, but the Museum also
has a sizable collection relating to the Edison Film Company.
However, its Collection is as nothing compared to the veri-
table treasure trove at the Edison National Historic Site (P.
O. Box 126, Orange, New Jersey 07051), whose vaults contain original scripts, glass negatives and legal papers, most
of which are as yet uncataloged. All the Site lacks is a
sizable collection of Edison films. Albert E. Smith, cofounder of the Vitagraph Company, maintained meticulous
business records, and these are now located, along with what
must be the only complete run in existence of the Vitagraph
Life Portrayals (1909-1916), in the Special Collections Division of the University of California, Los Angeles.

* This brief note first appeared in the Information Bulletin
of the International Federation of Film Archives (No. 6,
April, 1974). I have taken the opportunity afforded by its
reprinting here to update my findings.

In 1925, Vitagraph was purchased by Warner Brothers, and it seems highly probable that certain Vitagraph papers, along with some records of the Kalem Company, which Vitagraph had swallowed up earlier, may still be in existence at Warner's Burbank Studios. Warner Brothers neither confirms nor denies this.

Many film archives are now finding that the ideal way to persuade a film pioneer to part with his papers is to honor him with a film tribute. In 1947, the Academy of Motion Picture Arts and Sciences (8949 Wilshire Boulevard, Beverly Hills, Calif. 90211) presented a special Academy Award to, among others, Col. William Selig. He reciprocated by donating his papers to the Academy's Library. Other Selig material had been acquired from Charles G. Clarke of the American Society of Cinematographers, and he has now presented his collection to the Library, resulting in the Academy possessing an almost complete record of Selig productions. The Academy also owns the Mack Sennett Collection, which has recently been inventoried and is now accessible to researchers.

The University of Wyoming (Laramie, Wyoming) possesses some material relating to the Essanay Company, in particular a fine group of films donated by the widow of cofounder George K. Spoor. Materials on the Lubin Company are scattered. Much is held by the free library of Philadelphia (Logan Square, Philadelphia, Penn. 19102)--the Company was headquartered in Philadelphia--and Lubin's daughter, Emily Lowry, has certain papers, together with a wealth of memories. Harry and Roy Aitken were involved in many early companies--Reliance-Majestic, Keystone, Fine Arts, Epoch, etc.--and, thankfully, their papers have been donated to the Wisconsin Center for Theatre Research (Film Archive, 816 State Street, Madison, Wisconsin 53706).

RKO Radio Pictures began life in 1919 as Robertson-Cole, and today RKO's offices in Los Angeles house a massive collection of files, scripts, financial papers, etc. , covering the full history of the Company. It is to be hoped that one day these papers will be donated to a Library. Dorothy Devore was not only a leading lady with the Christie Comedy Company, but also a close personal friend of Al Christie. It was this friendship which resulted in Christie's bequeathing her his scripts and production schedules. I was able to arrange for the latter to go to the Library of Congress, while Miss Devore disposed of the scripts to the University of Wyoming. Aside from his fine work as an actor, Hobart Bos-

worth also ran his own production company, Bosworth, Inc.,
which later merged into Paramount, and today Bosworth's
widow maintains several rooms in her home in Palmdale,
California, as a memorial to her husband's career, each
room overflowing with unique research materials.

Distributor George Kleine's papers seem scattered
throughout the States. Some records are at the Library of
Congress, while still more are at the Academy Library.
Kleine, along with seven early production companies, formed
the Motion Picture Patents Company, whose legal records
for the years 1911-1915 are at the University of California,
Los Angeles. The Academy Library also has materials re-
lating to the Motion Picture Patents Company, donated by
Charles G. Clarke. Equally scattered are the files of pioneer
producer Thomas H. Ince, with the Academy, the Library of
Congress, the Museum of Modern Art and the University of
California, Los Angeles, all having sizable holdings.

Local historical societies are becoming increasingly
aware of the importance of recording local film history;
Rhode Island and New Mexico are excellent examples of societies that have set up local film history projects. Surprisingly, societies in major cities, such as Chicago, which one
would have imagined to have collected information on the two
major Chicago companies, Selig and Essanay, have nothing,
while small, obscure societies prove to have exciting finds.
One such society, the Wyoming Historical and Geological
Society (69 South Franklin Street, Wilkes-Barre, Penn. 18701)
holds the papers of pioneer showman Lyman Howe, together
with such esoteric items as a 1903 Selig Catalog.

In the tracking down of obscure film titles, particularly
films which were offered on a States Rights basis and in some
cases ignored by the trade papers, the records of local censorship boards are invaluable. A number of such boards
date back to the 'teens: Kansas, Maryland, Massachusetts
and New York. Unhappily, aside from the New York State
Censorship Board records, now preserved at the Manuscripts
and History Library of the New York State Library (The State
Education Department, Albany, N.Y. 12224), most of these
boards' files have been destroyed. However, some censorship boards, such as Kansas, did publish yearly reports and
approved and rejected motion pictures. The National Board
of review (founded in March, 1909, as the National Board of
Censorship) produced a quarterly catalog, delightfully titled
A Garden of American Motion Pictures for Father, Mother
and the Young People. These published records exist at

the Library of Congress, and, presumably, in a number of other major American libraries.

The personal papers of private individuals present a further source of information. Although, obviously, such materials are too numerous to note here, mention should be made of the William S. Hart papers at the Hart Ranch (Newhall, California) and further materials on Hart at the Library of Congress. The latter also possesses, in its Music Division, the papers of Geraldine Farrar. The Museum of Natural History of Los Angeles County (900 Exposition Boulevard, Los Angeles, Calif. 90007) owns the personal scrapbooks of the screen's two first leading ladies, Florence Lawrence and Florence Turner. Maurice Costello's pitiful effects are in the Library of the Academy of Motion Picture Arts and Sciences, and the scrapbooks of Selig actress Betty Harte are in the Library of the University of Southern California.

One of the major problems facing any researcher of this period of American film history is the lack of even remotely complete and accurate guides to collections. The two National Union Catalogs of Manuscript Collections and Serials do not list holdings in private libraries, such as the Academy of Motion Picture Arts and Sciences, and the former Catalog gives totally inadequate descriptions. American Theatrical Arts: A Guide to Manuscripts and Special Collections in the United States and Canada by William C. Young (Chicago: American Library Association, 1971) is helpful, but yet again far from complete in its listings. The International Federation of Film Archives has made a helpful contribution with its Union Catalog of Books and Periodicals Published Before 1914, but much more is needed, in particular a listing of holdings in private collections and non-member archives. One recent, pleasant development has been the preparation of Motion Pictures, Television and Radio; a Union Catalogue of Manuscript and Special Collections in the Western United States by the Los Angeles Film and Television Study Center. This catalogue, published in 1977 by G. K. Hall, includes all such collections housed in libraries and institutions in the eleven Western States. A similar volume covering the East Coast is planned.

INDEX